To Susan

Smile down inside yourself every day and the Universe will respond in kind. Wishing you all good times in the future.

Jessie

Jessie May Keesler
November 11, 2017

A BIRD AND THE DRAGON: THEIR LOVE STORY

A Memoir

JessieMay Kessler

BALBOA PRESS
A DIVISION OF HAY HOUSE

Copyright © 2016 JessieMay Kessler.

All rights reserved. No part of this book may be used or reproduced by any means, graphic, electronic, or mechanical, including photocopying, recording, taping or by any information storage retrieval system without the written permission of the author except in the case of brief quotations embodied in critical articles and reviews.

Balboa Press books may be ordered through booksellers or by contacting:

Balboa Press
A Division of Hay House
1663 Liberty Drive
Bloomington, IN 47403
www.balboapress.com
1 (877) 407-4847

Because of the dynamic nature of the Internet, any web addresses or links contained in this book may have changed since publication and may no longer be valid. The views expressed in this work are solely those of the author and do not necessarily reflect the views of the publisher, and the publisher hereby disclaims any responsibility for them.

The author of this book does not dispense medical advice or prescribe the use of any technique as a form of treatment for physical, emotional, or medical problems without the advice of a physician, either directly or indirectly. The intent of the author is only to offer information of a general nature to help you in your quest for emotional and spiritual well-being. In the event you use any of the information in this book for yourself, which is your constitutional right, the author and the publisher assume no responsibility for your actions.

Any people depicted in stock imagery provided by Thinkstock are models, and such images are being used for illustrative purposes only.
Certain stock imagery © Thinkstock.

Print information available on the last page.

ISBN: 978-1-5043-5145-4 (sc)
ISBN: 978-1-5043-5147-8 (hc)
ISBN: 978-1-5043-5146-1 (e)

Library of Congress Control Number: 2016907279

Balboa Press rev. date: 08/10/2016

CONTENTS

The Author's Explanation vii
The Dedication ix

Chapter 1:   The Meeting 1
Chapter 2:   A Mini Vacation 4
Chapter 3:   The First Date 7
Chapter 4:   Dating and Such 10
Chapter 5:   Meeting the Mothers 18
Chapter 6:   Halloween Escape 23
Chapter 7:   Who Wants a Ring 26
Chapter 8:   Meeting Custard 29
Chapter 9:   First Thanksgiving and Christmas 31
Chapter 10: To Find a House 34
Chapter 11: Moving Day 37
Chapter 12: Marching Toward a Wedding 39
Chapter 13: The Week of the Wedding 42
Chapter 14: The Wedding and Aftermath 44
Chapter 15: Drats! Reentry! 51
Chapter 16: The Shoe Box 54
Chapter 17: May 57
Chapter 18: Love Glue 62
Chapter 19: Nuts and Bolts 65
Chapter 20: Learning to Listen 69
Chapter 21: The Bottom Line 73
Chapter 22: Who's Running the House? 78
Chapter 23: Rocks in the Boat 83
Chapter 24: The Little Bird 86

Chapter 25: Time Alone 89
Chapter 26: Mile Stones 91
Chapter 27: Building a House 94
Chapter 28: Boyfriends 98
Chapter 29: The Book Store 104
Chapter 30: Transitions 111
Chapter 31: Letting Go for the New 119
Chapter 32: Lose Ends 122
Chapter 33: The Weddings 125
Chapter 34: The Cape Cottage 132
Chapter 35: New Life 135
Chapter 36: One More Lion 139
Chapter 37: A Life Changer 145
Chapter 38: Another Ending 149
Chapter 39: Weaving the Threads 152
Chapter 40: Making New Nests 156
Chapter 41: My Dragon 160
Chapter 42: It is Finished 169

Appendix I 177
Appendix II 179
Appendix III 183
The Author's Closing Remarks 185

THE AUTHOR'S EXPLANATION

A Bird and the Dragon: Their Love Story
A Memoir

Written by JessieMay Kessler
Started on October 20, 2014 eleven months after
my beloved husband,
Seymour Morris Kessler
died suddenly in hospital,
on November 20, 2013

THE DEDICATION

This book is dedicated
to all those couples
who, for better or worse,
give over parts of their lives
to raising their loved one's children,
created with someone else.
It is also dedicated to all the helpers
who stand and support these couples
in this complicated and incredible journey
of the blended family.

THE MEETING

Chapter One

I met my second husband, Sy, exactly one month, almost to the day, after my father, Frederick Copeland Sanderson, died of a lymphatic cancer. I have always felt that my father held on until he knew there was a knight coming to take over my protection, a responsibility that my father quietly carried in his heart from the day I was born. I said good bye to my father on a sticky, hot, July Wednesday and hello to my Sy on almost as hot a day, August 10, 1977. But before that there is back story.

I had been seeing a Jungian oriented psychotherapist for about two years as I prepared to strengthen myself to the point where I could ask my then husband, the Rev. Harvard Lesser, for a divorce. We had come to the point where it was apparent to me that no amount of counseling would bring us onto the same page and so it was time to move on. But enough on that subject!

In June of 1977 I was living alone in the marital family home with my three girls, May, Elizabeth,(Kitty) and Felicia (Happy). I had been alone since a year ago March, handling all of the domestic details and living somewhere between shock and depression. In June, May began acting up, challenging my authority. I was in a session with Rev. David Eaton, my therapist, giving him my rendition of the troubles with May. Toward the end of the session he told me that there was a gentleman about my age that he had been counseling and he wondered if he could give the man my telephone number. Still in my state of agitation over May, I flippantly said, "Sure, give him my name, telephone number, measurements. Whatever he wants!" The session ended and I was on my way.

Weeks later I had not had a telephone call from any perspective gentleman and was sitting in my office feeling sorry for myself. I took out the telephone book and looked through it until I found a Seymour Kessler listed in Nerme, Connecticut, the town where David had told me the man lived. I sat with the telephone book open in my lap wondering what a Jewish man with that sort of name would look like. Quickly a short, bald headed man with a typical paunch appeared, I think he had glasses and I thought, "Oh, well, David said that the religion would not be an issue." Next thing I knew I saw a road in front of me running up an incline and bending to the left. The street was lined with trees and there were houses on each side. I thought, now that is just too weird, and closed the telephone book.

Somewhere towards the end of July, David mentioned that he felt I was healed enough that I should think about graduation and terminating my individual sessions with him. I was taken aback because I had not thought about a life without David's steady support. As diversion I said, "So what happened? Didn't you give my telephone number to the gentleman you mentioned?" And David responded, "No I didn't give him your number because from your reply I didn't think you were ready for a new relationship." I was crushed because I knew I'd shot myself in the foot and couldn't really complain. The session came to a close and I returned to home and the girls.

At the next session with David he asked if I'd given any thought to graduation and I froze. He said, "I've been thinking about your situation and I'm starting a group for divorcing singles and wondered if you would like to join it as a stepping stone to your independence."

'Ah,' I thought, 'a light in the darkness ahead.' "Yes, I'd like to join the group," I responded. And we continued with the session.

Just as David was ushering me out the door he said, "Oh, and by the way, Seymour is going to be a part of that group."

So now to August 10th 1977.

As I said before, it was a hot day in August and the day's chores were mostly complete at home, as if the chores in any household with children are ever completed. I'd gotten supper for the girls and had them ready for the baby sitter. They were acting up and being difficult and I felt rushed, excited, and not prepared. I yelled at them and grabbed my purse just as the baby sitter arrived. I gave instructions and bolted out the door to the car knowing that I would be late.

As I pulled into the drive at David's house there were other cars there. This surprised me since always before I was the only one sharing David's home. I walked up to the front door, which was open, and wished I could turn around and run. By now I was thinking I don't want to meet a balding, paunchy Jewish man and I've never much felt comfortable in a group of people.

David opened the screen door and motioned me to come in and join the other people in the living room. There were both men and women seated in chairs and on the couch. Since I was hot and the breeze was moving the curtains behind it, I chose to sit on the corner of the couch. David stepped back to the screen door and then called to those of us waiting, "Most everyone is here. We are just waiting for Sy Kessler." That was a relief because none of the men in the room were short, balding or paunchy.

"Ah, here he is," David announced. In what seemed like one simple movement, a tall, physically trim man with curly brown hair stepped to the door of the living room. "Here is Sy Kessler," David announced. I stared at the man before me. He had sideburns, plenty of brown curly hair and a somewhat self-effacing grin. 'He's a rebel,' I thought. 'He's a rebel just like me!'

I don't remember much more about that first meeting at David's house. I know we all filed down to his basement office and sat around on chairs, straight and overstuffed, along with a couple of bean bag chairs. There were introductions and I began to realize these people were all struggling with issues similar to mine. There was really no reason to be scared or unable to talk and share my story.

A MINI VACATION

Chapter Two

It had to be two weeks into our group meetings at David's house and we had all had a chance to share our stories. Sy was an engineer working in the sonar division for a company known as The Lab in Whaling City, Connecticut, helping to improve our nation's submarines, a government job that was often top secret. He had been married for fifteen years to a young woman he had met during his college days. According to him she was an alcoholic and, more often than not, by the time he got home from work she was not able to prepare the evening meal or take care of their two daughters.

Other people shared their stories, but it was Sy's story that I was soaking up, wanting to understand everything I could about this intriguing man. Toward the end of that second session Sy announced that he and his wife's parents were taking the girls on a week's vacation to an animal reserve in upper state New York. He wouldn't be at the next meeting. That was one of the longest periods in my life, along with the first week he went to sea for submarine testing after we were married, and this past year, since his death.

Two weeks later, when he returned to the group, I got my courage up to ask if he had enjoyed his time away with his girls and he said that it was great to be free of the uncertainties of his troubled marriage and the pressures of work.

I was so excited. I'd actually managed to speak to him and he took me seriously and answered me with his soft but well-articulated, slightly Bronx New York accent. I wasn't used to being treated as if what I had to say meant anything.

The following week, towards the end of the discussion, we were all sharing some of the things that were the most difficult for each of us. I'd managed to find a seat beside Sy and was listening intently when he said, "The hardest time for me is when I get home from work, round up the girls, get them started on their homework, cook dinner, such as it is, and then have to send them for baths, and tuck them into bed. When that's done I finish cleaning up the kitchen, get out the newspaper, find my slippers and sit down to read. Then it hits me. I'm all alone. I'm all alone with these girls and totally responsible for their well-being. Not that I haven't been alone with them before, but this is different!"

Without even thinking, I leaned forward and put my hand on his thigh. "That's the same way it is for me. I've always been the responsible one, but now I'm all alone with these children." Suddenly, realizing I'd invaded his space, I went to pull my hand back and he closed his large strong left hand over mine squeezing it slightly before he let me retreat. That moment was like a bolt of lightning passing between us. The intensity of the energy was unmistakable.

The following meeting came just before Labor Day. We spent the evening talking about our hopes and needs for the future and how we could go about getting some of those needs met. One of the female participants must have taken the conversation literally because she said, "I don't know about the rest of you but I find this group cold and I feel cold. I need to hug people." With that she got up and started around to the members, handing out hugs. When she got to Sy, who was at the end of the circle, she said, "And your bean bag chair looks so comfy I'm going to sit right here." Sy, never one to reject or protest, sort of tucked her under his arm and they finished the meeting this way. I'm seething by now because in my mind he belongs to me after his response at the last meeting. When the session was over I heard her ask Sy if he wanted to go for coffee and a bite to eat. I wormed my way to the head of the people going up the cellar stairs and made my way straight to the kitchen and David's wife Jodie. I'm standing behind her as my fellow group members pass by the kitchen—Sy in tow of this encroaching lady.

When David appeared he said to me, "What's wrong?"

I sputtered, "There goes Sy with that woman!"

David turned as if he could still see them and then back to me. "I think it's just for coffee," he said.

Coffee, beer, whatever, that woman was moving in on the best man I'd met in a long time and in my heart he was mine. The days out ahead of me looked bleak.

THE FIRST DATE

Chapter Three

It took me suffering from Wednesday to Friday night and then I knew I had to do something before Sy slid right out of my life. I paced, and deliberated, argued with myself as to whether this was appropriate or not, and came back to, "I can't lose him." Mid-morning on Saturday I picked up the telephone, an instrument I have disliked ever since I was a child and, you remember, I had his telephone number from my encounter with the telephone book during the summer. I dialed his number and then prayed that he'd answer it, no, that he wouldn't answer it, yes, that he would answer it. His steady voice came on the other end as I fumbled with who I was and what I wanted. "This is Jessie from our divorce group and I'm taking my girls swimming this afternoon. I wondered if you'd like to come and bring your girls and we all go swimming together." Without a moment's hesitation he responded, "That sounds like a great idea. What time would you want us at your house?" Who cared about the time--he had said yes!! I suggested around 1:00 p.m., I guess. I don't remember now.

The hour before they arrived my two girls had been grilling me on who these strange people were going to be, and why we were all going swimming, and as long as it was swimming it would be okay. I had given Sy detailed directions and when he arrived with his daughters, Cora, 13 and Annie, 8 they came to the back door of the house. Hobo, our beloved old tan Welch Corgi was stretched out over the cement landing at the back door. Sy stepped close to the door but talked through the screen to me. He drew his girls in closer to him and introduced them. Meanwhile the dog lay motionless in his position as guard dog outside the back door. When I finally opened the screen door, Sy stepped over the dog and the two girls followed their father. Hobo lifted his head ever so slightly and wagged his tail. In that instant I thought, 'He approves and he has just allowed this family into my life.'

Hobo was right. Sy chose where we should go swimming and at that point I was so full of happiness I didn't care where we went. At first the girls eyed each other, but gradually, with our encouragement they began to talk, and finally, to walk out into the lake. Soon they were calling for us to come join them. Sy and I walked into the cold water and played for a while with the girls but we really wanted to talk to each other so we would gravitate toward one another. The girls caught on quickly to what was up and they would pull on each parent respectively to try to keep us from getting together. Finally, in desperation Sy said, "You girls stay out here and play, while Jessie and I go in and talk on the beach. And remember, nobody goes into the water above their chest." Oh, such a comfort I thought--the man of the house making the rules.

And right now, I can hear his voice from the other side saying, "And tell them about the black bikini." Back then I had a figure and a small black bikini. I believe he always thought it was the black bikini that captured his heart, at least that is what he would tell people, but I know there really was more.

I cannot remember what we talked about. I do know that occasionally Sy had to call out to one or the other of the children that they were in too deep. And by the end of the afternoon he was beginning to finish my sentences and I was finishing his thoughts. "This is strange," Sy said. "It feels like I've known you for years." I had to agree. I tend to be shy and that was not part of that afternoon. Whatever I wanted to say to him just came rolling out and he was accepting, listening, and adding to my ideas.

As it began to get late we called the girls into the shore for towels and Sy asked if they wanted to go home or go out to eat at a restaurant. Being girls, they, with one voice said, "Out to eat!" So we gathered wet children and headed to my home to find dry clothes. We ended up at a little restaurant, a sandwich ice cream shop in Grows Town, which has long since been replaced with newer eateries, but it was clean, well-lit and what we needed. The girls walked up the aisles and picked a booth that the four of them could cram into and then pointed to us to take the booth in front of them.

There was some quibbling over the menu and who would have what, but for girls that had never met before, they really did give us some time to enjoy each other as they laughed and giggled in their booth.

All of the authoritative books on dating for the second time say not to let the children know until you know that the relationship is going to work, but we didn't seem to have a choice and the girls themselves so quickly showed us that we needed each other to make a family together. Yes, there were bumps and wiggles and lumps in the rug, but as the story goes on we found ways of making it work. It was only a week later when we had planned a walk at the Whaling City arboretum. As we were driving away from our walk, Annie, the youngest of the girls, leaned over our bench seat in the car (back then they were bench seats) and said, "When are you two getting married?" She knew, perhaps before we did, that this was a forever match.

DATING AND SUCH

Chapter Four

Labor Day

I believe Labor Day that year was two days after that first swimming date. Sy called early in the morning and asked if I and my girls would like to come over to his house later in the afternoon for a cook out picnic. The girls could play and we would get in some serious talking. Since he was making the invitation he volunteered to come and get us and return us in the early evening.

It sounded like a great plan to me and I told my girls about Sy's suggestion and to get their rooms picked up and ready for our afternoon invitation. They seemed excited this time.

Sy rounded us up and had driven into Nerme Village and turned off route 100 going toward his house. He then took a quick right and there we were going up the little hill I had seen when I was holding the telephone book earlier that summer. In disbelief I blurted out, "I've been here before. Well, not really, but I have."

"What are you talking about?" Sy asked from behind the wheel. I was embarrassed and a bit confused, but I told him the story in brief as we were approaching the house. "That is strange," he said in response to my tale. Little did he know that he had a life time of those "strange" things ahead of him.

It was a beautiful autumn day with sunshine and that crisp odor that belongs only to autumn. It was still warm enough that the children were happy to spend their last free day outside playing. They were off and about in the yard and into the house and out again. We sat drinking a cocktail that Sy had prepared and talked. I can't remember all of the conversation of course—it was thirty seven years ago, now. But what I do remember is that the conversation got to some deep places and at one point he made a confession about something very personal to him. I was taken aback that he would share with me so soon such personal material and yet I was over joyed that he trusted me that much. It helped to cement the already fast growing fire between us.

When it was time for clean-up, Sy and I were in his kitchen while the girls were somewhere in the large house playing a game they had concocted. The dishes were washed, the counters cleaned, the food put away—most of it Sy's doing, and we could feel the date growing to its natural close. Sy reached down and drew me to him and as I nestled into his arms I could smell that his masculine scent was the same as my father's and my body relaxed into comfort. He leaned down and kissed me. Not expecting that, I pulled back a bit and saw the kitchen clock over his shoulder with its hands spinning in circles. I snuggled back into his arms as we heard Cora calling, "Daddy…Daddy we need…Oh, excuse me. I didn't know," she offered as she bombed into the room. We assured her that her behavior was okay, as indeed it was. We both had the answers we needed by then to move forward.

The Practical Joke

This period in our romance lasted from Labor Day until February 25, 1978—the day we were married. So instead of one large memory there are many little ones, some of which I will share.

We did a lot of lunch dates to have private time away from the curious eyes of the girls. One I remember vividly. We had been talking on the telephone during the evenings and any time we could catch on a week end, but this was a lunch date. Sy invited me to a family restaurant in Whaling City and I met him there. I was late as usual so I was feeling a little off kilter, already. He assured me that I wasn't all that late and we sat down and took the large menus offered by the waitress. I was buried in mine trying, to focus on the extensive menu, and Sy was tucked behind his, still talking to me. Suddenly, I caught the words, "I was thinking that maybe we should slow this down a bit, maybe not see so much of each other."

I went cold in my seat. I couldn't find any words, the writing on the menu disappeared, and the tears started rolling down my cheeks.

By now he had dropped his menu a bit, looking, I suppose, for a reaction and saw that I was crying. "Are you okay," he asked?

"No, I'm not okay. I didn't know you felt that way," were the only words that came.

"Oh, Honey, I was joking with you. I didn't really mean it. It was just a practical joke!"

Between clenched teeth I responded, "It wasn't a joke to me. I don't do jokes well and that really hurt. Don't ever say something like that to me again unless you mean it."

He shifted in his seat and leaned in toward me. "Forgive me? I will never ever say something so hurtful to you again." And he has been true to his word for thirty-six years.

The Hot Lobster Roll

The weather was still warm on one of those rare October days that feel like summer has returned. Sy invited me to meet him in Whaling City for a hot lobster roll at a little restaurant on Main Street back before the town turned the main street into a walking mall. I was to meet him in a near-by parking lot. I got out of the car and visually searched for him. He was standing on the far corner in the bright sunshine and had on his blue jean jacket with the cuffs turned back and the collar turned up in the back, reminiscent of the late 1950's, early 60's. I thought to myself as I walked toward him, 'He is incredibly handsome. He stands so erect, with quantities of brown curly hair combed back in an effort to control the look. I want to hold this picture forever,' and I have. It was also one of my first times of knowing beyond a shadow of a doubt that this was the man I wanted to spend the rest of my life with.

We had our buttery, drooling lobster rolls—the best I have ever eaten--licked our fingers and then he apparently didn't want to go back to work any more than I wanted to go back to housekeeping. He suggested I follow him and he drove out along the river until he came to Heritage Park and turned into the parking lot. "Want to walk a bit?" he asked through my car window. "The gardens are dying down but they are still nice to look at."

"I've never been here before," I responded. At least I couldn't remember being there during the time I was with Harvard. He and I seemed to mostly be embroiled in church work and raising small children.

Sy led me down into the back gardens and the great sunny lawn sprawling out before us with the glistening ocean even farther beyond. I assume we talked but mostly what I remember is his holding my hand in a steady grip and guiding me through the gardens to the lawn. The wind had picked up in this location so we sought out a sunny place protected by bushes. We sat talking for a bit and then it was time to be heading back to the real world. I think it was on this day that he said, "It's time to start putting the girls together on weekends so that we can feel how this is going to work, moving forward."

We did put the girls together every weekend at my home in Grows Town, through Christmas and beyond. My memory is that it rained the first seven weekends in a row and we both said that if we could get through this together we could get through anything. Little did we know how many 'anythings' were ahead.

The Night Gown

I can't remember which house we were in but I'm assuming that it was after we started spending the weekends together with all the girls as chaperones. Sy said he had a gift for me and I was surprised, but pleased. What girl doesn't like a surprise gift? He took from behind his back a blouse sized box nicely wrapped in feminine colored paper. "What's in it?" I teased.

He nodded to move on and said, "Open it and you'll see."

I tried my Christmas pulling-the-scotch-tape-off-slowly first and he said, "No, just open it!"

Inside the box was a tan colored light weight flannel type nightie with a lace collar and brown and aqua flowers embroidered on the collar and a sheer nylon area just below the collar. It was floor length and had push up sleeves with elastic at the cuffs.

I couldn't believe my eyes because at that point he hadn't asked me to marry him and a nightie seemed a bit presumptuous.

He must have read my mind because his next words were, "I know it is pretty early in our relationship but I saw it in the store and it looked like you. I hope you don't think I'm being too forward."

"No, you are not being too forward; I'm amazed at how you already know what would be in my taste. We haven't been together that long."

"I watch," he said. And that has been his hallmark all these years; he always watched to see what would please others and then set out to do his best to make it happen.

When the time comes that my girls are packing up and giving away my things they will find at the bottom of a drawer or in a box in the closet a well-worn nightie with brown and aqua flowers embroidered on the front—my first gift from Sy.

The Green Monster

One of the events ahead was the evening we decided to go out to dinner and leave all the girls with a baby sitter who was used to watching my three girls. (My adopted daughter, May, was also included in these group events although she was living the rest of the time with her father on the far side of the block behind the family home.) May was always the child who thought up the mischief, and before Sy got there, the girls were throwing food at each other in the kitchen while I tried to dress for my date. I could see them and was growing increasingly annoyed. Finally, I marched out to the kitchen and said, "This isn't fair. I spend every day of my life with you, taking care of you and now this is my time to go out and play and you are trying to stop me from going. Do you really want to destroy my date?" They looked stunned and one of them mumbled; "No." and they settle down and ate the rest of their supper.

I should have known, but I so wanted a few hours with Sy. The baby sitter arrived and got her instructions. Sy arrived, we said 'good bye and be good' to all the girls, and left.

As we were returning from our wonderful dinner out, we could see police car lights or was it ambulance lights somewhere in the vicinity of my house. Getting closer we saw that it was police and their flashers were indeed going. May had apparently managed to make herself black out or something similar and it terrified everyone in the house so they called the police and they in turn called the ambulance. My memory is foggy, but I don't think they actually took her to the hospital. The men on duty put it together that this was protest or attention getting because the parents were out on a date. Whatever the outcome, May went quickly back to her father's and gained no positive points with her potential new step-father, Sy.

Do You Love Me

I have already mentioned that it rained for seven weekends in a row and along about the seventh the girls had gotten into a routine of who played what with whom. Sy was busy fixing one of the things that Harvard had left on the To-do list and I was in the girl's bathroom scrubbing out the bathtub. Cora came in and perched on the side of the tub as I worked. We talked about several things and then she said to me, "Do you love me?" Taken aback by her question, my mind raced to weigh my options. Should I tell her what she wanted to hear or should I tell her the truth and how would she take that? What I said was, "Cora, no I don't love you, now. I have only known you for a little over eight weeks. But I love your father very much and he loves you, so I expect in time I will love you, also."

She looked like I had hit her with my wet cloth and then she began to scream as only a thirteen year old girl can do, "You don't love me! How can you not love me? I hate you!" and raced out of the bathroom and toward the room where she was sleeping with the others. Her screams were loud enough to wake anyone trying to sleep in that split level house.

I knew her father could hear her and I had better do something quick! Instead of going to Cora to try to comfort her, I went to Sy and explained what had happened. He was still for a moment and then he said, "What else could you have said to her? If you told her you loved her she would never trust you in the future. Saying what you did hurt her for now but it opens the door for her to love you later on." Time has proven him to be absolutely right. Today she and I talk back and forth freely about whatever.

She also was the daughter that taught me it is safe to openly fight with your children when there are festering issues.

The Yellow Rose Buds

Sy spent Thursday evening, October 12, 1977, with me. I think he brought his girls to my house. My divorce was to be final the next day and he sensed that I was agitated, maybe even a little afraid of what that day might bring. At some previous time, probably on a weekend together, I had been playing hymns and singing to him. I showed him the hymn "Morning Has Broken" and said, "I really love this song because it speaks to the way I feel about you and our new life together." He listened and agreed that the words and melody fit what was happening to us.

We said our good-byes at the end of the evening, he headed to Nerme and I trotted off to bed. The next morning, as I fished for the alarm clock, I saw there was a greeting card in an envelope on my side table. I sat up and opened it. The picture was all in yellows and there were green trees and birds singing, and those beautiful words from "Morning Has Broken" written inside. He had added, "Know that I am with you no matter what happens, I will love you always, Sy."

What happened was incredulous. I arrived at the court house in Thames City, Connecticut and my lawyer, Paul Stanford, was there, Harvard and his lawyer were there, and Paul motioned for me to have a seat in the hall. We waited. Then later he came to me, bent down, and whispered in my ear, "Harvard is counter suing you for the Grows Town house, custody of the girls, and all of the assets."

In consternation I blurted out, "He can't do that! The agreement was amical and already signed by both of us."

Paul responded, "Oh, yes he can, but we are going to make short work of this, his lawyer and I. You go sit in that office over there and wait until we lawyers work this through. I will come for you when we are done."

About forty-five minutes later Paul came to get me. Knowing what I would be asking, he said, "It has all been taken care of and we need to go into the court room, now. The Judge is going to ask you if this is an irreconcilable break down of the marriage and you simply answer, 'Yes.'"

I did as I was told and for much of it, I must have been in shock because I don't remember any more details until I finally returned home in the early afternoon. I parked the car at the back of the house and as I looked up I could see Sy was sitting on the concrete steps with flowers in his hands. I was surprised to see him since I thought he was at work, and as I approached him he stood up, gathered me in with one arm, kissed me firmly, and then handed me a bouquet of twelve yellow rose buds still wrapped tightly within themselves.

"Oh, they are so beautiful!" I exclaimed, while thinking to myself what a perfect representation of our relationship.

We went into the house and I guess I offered Sy coffee to my cup of tea. I told him about the dreadful time in court and when I had finally gotten my story out, I noticed he was looking at me as if I had forgotten something. I hadn't forgotten; I was thrown by what had gone on in court. It felt as if I had just lifted one foot from the old wooden dock and was about to put the other foot into a new row boat. I had not wanted to be physically intimate with Sy until I knew that I was legally divorced. And Harvard, thinking that I would change my mind, was dragging things out in terms of moving forward with the divorce. I think if Sy had not come upon the stage, Harvard might have let the divorce dangle forever. Sy and I had made the agreement that there would be no intimacy until my divorce was final or Thanksgiving arrived—whichever came first. He was very respectful of my request. We did take the relationship forward that afternoon and the yellow roses have come to symbolize many things between us. I put fully opened yellow roses on the altar the day of his memorial service. I knew he would understand what they meant. I have pressed one and it is in his memorial book.

MEETING THE MOTHERS

Chapter Five

Meeting my mother was not as amusing as what led up to the meeting between Sy and my mother. It was becoming increasingly obvious that our relationship was headed for a long term route. So on a visit back to my mother's house when she still lived up on the hill outside the front gate of the Industrial School in Shakerton, Massachusetts, I thought I'd better start giving her more specifics about this new man in my life.

We were sitting at the big, pine, drop-leaf harvest table that warmed her family room/kitchen. I hadn't been home for a while—I had been busy getting to know Sy. Mother was doing the talking and I was listening. She talked about the church supper coming up and that she would be doing the set up while her friend, Dorris, did much of the kitchen work. Right in the middle of a sentence she reached out and patted my hand. "Now, you tell me about this new man!" she said. "What's his name?"

Knowing my mother, I hesitated for a moment and then I said, "His name is Seymour Morris Kessler."

There was that pregnant pause and then my mother said, "Oh, my Dear, I hope he is not another robin with a broken wing." I knew she was referring to my tendency to choose men who need some bolstering or for lack of a better word, some emotional support. --Okay, I'm a rescuer.

"Mom, this man is not a robin and he has a pair of gorgeous wings. You'll see when you meet him," I assured her.

"Well, I do hope so. You have had such bad luck up to now. Let's set a date to meet him. Maybe, for a lunch?" The date was set and the conversation went on for much of the afternoon.

The day came and I don't remember how we arranged it, but we were without children. The autumn air was clear and the sun was bright. I was almost giddy with anticipation because I knew this time my mother would like my choice. We drove from Grows Town, Connecticut, and as we were getting near the town of Shakerton, Sy asked if I knew of a gas station where he could stop because he was so nervous. We found one in Boynton, Massachusetts. He relieved himself but when he came back out to the car he said, "I have a question to ask you."

"Okay," I responded wondering what could have happened in the men's room to make him so serious.

"Before we meet your mother I need to ask you, will you marry me?"

I was dumb founded. I knew the question would come, just not on this particular day. And he hadn't yet met my mother. That could change everything or it might for some people.

Before he could rethink or restate his question I said, "Oh, yes, I can't even envision a life without you." We hugged and kissed and then we drove on with him asking questions about my mother and my trying to feed him information that would help to lower the anxiety. The topic of lunch came up and he said he could handle most anything but tuna casserole. I assured him that I couldn't remember my mother ever making a tuna casserole.

We arrived at the house I left when I was eighteen years old, and my mother greeted both of us with that warm enthusiasm that made my mother the sunshine in my life. She asked him questions and he must have answered correctly because she let him marry me. After a bit she said, "Now the food is just about ready. I made you a lovely, cheesy tuna casserole for lunch." We looked at each other but she missed the exchange. I had forgotten that my mother had a knack for finding the underbelly, because she had done the same thing to my brother-in-law when my sister first brought him home. She served Bud everything that he didn't like. Thankfully this time there was plenty of cheese and I still make that casserole occasionally, today.

There are bits and pieces of my mother and Sy that are very similar—astrologically they are both Leos and Sy was born on the birth date of my mother's mother, Mary Emma Gould Moody, August 22. So he already had a foot in the door. They chatted. She tried to find out specifics graciously, and he nicely avoided the answers, which I think pleased her because she could see he was an intelligent, loyal man, with his priorities in the right order.

As I said in the beginning of this tale, my father died a month before I had meet Sy and not knowing how my Love would ever know my father I asked Sy if he would like to walk with me down to my father's gravesite to meet him. Sy said he would. So we started out walking toward the town, talking and holding hands and I suppose dreaming out loud about our future, which we both felt had already been blessed by my mother. We turned into the village cemetery and I spoke about the different families that had engraved headstones along our route. I told Sy about those that I knew and then suddenly we were standing at my father's gravesite. With a little embarrassment I said, "Sy, this is my father, Frederick Copeland Sanderson, and Dad, this is my intended, Sy Kessler." I felt Sy squeeze my hand harder than usual. I looked up to see that tears were rolling down his cheeks. He made no effort to hide them or to explain. And I knew the tears were not so much for meeting my father as they were for missing his own father who died when Sy was only seven years old, leaving him to grow up without a paternal mentor and friend. He has had to invent what a father should be and he has done a remarkable job.

When he seemed composed again we started the walk back to my mother's house and we have never spoken about the tears. There was never a need to because we both understood why they were there.

It had to have been some time in the next week when Sy called me in the evening and said he was taking a long lunch the next day and, "Can you come and meet my mother?" Of course I would be pleased to meet his mother. It was only fair. I knew that he had mixed feelings about her but that he had always felt responsible for her wellbeing, as the last living son of two. At some point before I met Sy, he had moved Celia from her home in the outskirts of New York City to Whaling City, Connecticut where he could better get to her when she needed help. She rented an apartment in one of the high rise buildings, certainly a smaller space than she was used to and I think perhaps in a poorer neighborhood. Both Sy and his mother were frugal people and the environment may have transpired out of what could be afforded.

I remember riding up in the elevator and smelling the boiled cabbage and hamburger. Sy leaned into me and said, "That's one of the things I have always hated about city living."

I clutched his hand as we walked down the hall toward the door of her apartment. I'd never even seen a picture of her and now I was about to meet my future mother-in-law. She was a small sturdy Polish woman with gray/white thinning hair combed back to create an exposed face—practical and down to earth. She gave me a hug and then gestured for us to come into her tiny apartment. The entrance was small enough that Sy and I had trouble stepping around her. I was first in and looked across her sitting room to the large window looking over the city. The light was dim, but strong enough for me to be struck with all the Italian type bric-a-brac on the side tables, the marble pillars with tiny statues, the silk flowers that were dusty. It seemed as if every space was filled. And the same Italian flavored pictures hung on the walls. It was as if it had never been updated.

Celia was cordial but not warm in her conversation with me. She said all the gracious things but you didn't feel any open arms as I think Sy did with my mother. I can't remember how the conversation went; I think because she talked mostly to Sy about things she needed him to do for her.

When we were back in the hall Sy just looked at me, but didn't ask for an evaluation. The evaluation came in the middle of that ensuing night. In my bed, I couldn't fall asleep because I was troubling over the tremendous difference in Sy and his sophisticated taste, and what I saw in his mother's apartment. Her apartment looked like homes I had visited as a girl, homes in the town of Shakerton that belonged to the French Canadian or Polish factory workers. According to my mother they were "the other people" in the town. Was my Sy one of these? He didn't feel that way to me. Then somehow as I was falling asleep the words came to me—Celia is very like your father, steadfast, no frills, caught in the past and very rooted to the earth. With that I heaved a sigh of relief and fell asleep.

My assessment of my mother-in-law was accurate and, although we didn't talk a lot, she did fill me in on her history of being sent to this country at seventeen, alone, at the time of the build up to World War II. Her brothers were here in this country and her father, no longer having a wife to help raise a daughter, had sent Celia to one of them in New York City to get her out of war torn Poland. She was not trained for employment but wound up taking care of the young man who was ill across the street. The young man, Leo Siciliano married her some time later and they had two sons, Paul and Seymour. Sy's father worked in a tie factory as did Celia. It was when Sy was five years old that Leo started coming home late to dinner, and being the practical person she was, Celia followed him one evening and confronted him in the bed of another woman. He was out of the family home with his things in the street before he knew what hit him, and Celia sued him for divorce, changing the boy's surname to her own, Kessler.

As I said, we didn't chat a lot, but I had the same quiet understanding of her that I had with my father. Steady, warm hearted, always there, just not able to emote about feelings.

HALLOWEEN ESCAPE

Chapter Six

Now that my mother was aware of how serious we were, I knew that everyone in my extended family would know and I wanted them to make their own judgments. So we decided we would take the Halloween weekend and drive north to Vermont to introduce Sy to my sister PollyAnne and her husband, Bud, along with an assortment of their children.

It is no small task to find someone who is willing to devote their whole weekend to supervising, entertaining, and feeding four active girls. We called everyone that we could think of, including my mother, but she was busy with another church supper. (I bet she was glad!) Finally, Sy's in-laws, Joe and Bootsie Baker, said they could take the girls. With many misgivings, we packed up four of our five daughters--the fifth stayed with her father--and drove them up to South Winston, Connecticut. Sy's in-laws had moved from the family home on the corner of route 30 and 107 to a smaller place with a pond. Cora and Annie were right at home, but my girls held back until Gamma Bootsie came up with some brilliant plan to engage all of them--probably, jumping into a giant pile of leaves.

The girls were accounted for! But what to do with the dog, Hobo? Nobody wanted an old, scruffy, good natured dog with short legs and a big head. Only one solution—we had to take him with us. We packed our suit cases and food for Hobo and started out. It was so late in the day by the time everyone was accounted for that we only got to Brattleboro, Vermont, that first night. We found a motel that would take Hobo, fed him, parked our belongings and went out to supper. Never having taken Hobo on the road, contrary to his name, I was afraid he might howl.

But he was good as gold and greeted us with a wagging tail when we got back. We watched some television, talked, showered, and fell into bed. I'd put Hobo's bedding on the floor by my side of the bed because he was accustomed to that spot. Somewhere around 3:00 a.m. I heard rustling. I opened my eyes enough, that with the light shining in from a street sign, I could see that Hobo was no longer beside me. Propping up on one elbow, I saw Sy standing at the bottom of the bed tugging on a shirt. I lay down and made like I was asleep. When they came back in through the sliding glass doors, I rolled over and said, "What happened? Are you both okay?" Sy unclipped Hobo from his leash, took off the shirt, and slid into bed beside me. "Hobo just had to pee," he said and settled down to sleep. I couldn't resist. "He's a smart dog," I said. I heard a slightly disgruntled, "You got that right!" from the other side of the bed.

We three managed to make it to PollyAnne's farm in central Vermont the next morning. My sister and her husband greeted Sy with enthusiasm—my mother had obviously beaten me to the telephone. They served a nice lunch and we got to meet some of their children-- Marie, Tom (the boyfriend), Beth and Eddie. I can't remember if Holly, the oldest daughter, was already out of the home. Maybe she was at college in Bunker City at that time. We adults talked for a lot of the afternoon, the conversation punctuated by their Doberman Pincer, tied to the leg of the family room couch, growling at Hobo. Hobo lay beside me closer to the door and would calmly wag his tail now and then. I suspect Sy was taken out to the barn by Bud to see his cows and to let Bud get a feel for who Sy was since Bud and I had always been close and he would want to warn me if things didn't feel right.

I remember feeling so content and so exhausted Sunday morning when I woke up because I couldn't sleep on the bed in the upstairs bedroom. My delicate nature wanted my own hard, flat, bed back home. This bed was concaved and I tried clinging to the edge but would roll into Sy and then have to pull myself back to the outer edge. I finally tucked a leg over the side and managed to let him sleep in peace for some time. But the contentment came from knowing that this man was being accepted by my family. I'm not sure we did much that Sunday morning but to eat and talk more.

A Bird and the Dragon: Their Love Story

At some point in the journey I remember being delighted with the colors of the trees. Some friend back home had told us that it wasn't really worth going north on Halloween weekend to see the foliage because it would be brown. They didn't know that at this stage in our relationship all the trees were crimson, gold, salmon pink, and sparkling.

We picked the girls up and listened to their various tales of adventure while we drove toward home. By then, for me, it was a rosy haze of fatigue and pleasure.

*Our Starting Family:
Back row: Kitty, Sy and Cora
Front row: Happy, Jessie and Annie*

WHO WANTS A RING

Chapter Seven

Introductions to the rest of my family would come later. Sy and I had talked about getting engaged and I explained that I wanted to be engaged, but I didn't want a ring. When I became engaged to Rev. Harvard Lesser, he had given me a lovely large diamond with two side chips which created an eye-catching ring, but after I received it, he confessed that he had been engaged before and this was the ring. I was hurt, but in those days I was too timid to show my feelings. Instead I asked him to change the band to a yellow gold so that it would fit with the eventual traditional wedding band. I guess, at some level, he recognized the misstep and quickly had the ring refashioned from the white gold band to a golden yellow band. The setting of course was still the same in the white gold. Over the years I grew to see that the whole episode pointed to some of the things that made us incompatible.

Sy listened to my story and understood. If I didn't want a ring, what did I want? "Could I have earrings instead? Maybe they could be in my birth stone or whatever you feel is right," I said. We were still attending the divorce group and he usually came and got me and drove both of us to the meetings on Wednesday evening. But this was a Tuesday night, the night before, and he called and wanted to take me out for a little while. Any excuse to be with him was wonderful to me. After we started out in the direction we would have gone to the meeting, he pulled off of route 185 at his exit as if we were going to his house. He swung into a parking lot at the base of route 185 by the overpass of the highway. At that point I had no idea why we were in a parking lot instead of going to get something to eat or going down to the ocean. He parked the car, leaned over and kissed me, his hands on each shoulder like it was important. Then he told me to close my eyes. I felt him put a small box into my hand. "Okay, open your eyes!" he said. I did and found I was holding a tiny jeweler's box wrapped in gray velvet. "Open it," he commanded, his enthusiasm showing in his voice. When I opened the box there were two amethyst stud earrings in an exquisite shade of purple resting inside the box. "Put them on," he said gently. "Let's see if they are right."

"Oh, Honey, they are perfect. I would have picked them if I had been with you!" I told him as I tried to put them on, but I was so excited that my hands shook, and then I found that the opening in my earlobe was closed from lack of use. "I'll have to open the holes at home with hot water," I said. "Can you wait?"

"I'm not sure. But you agree we are officially engaged as of tonight?"

"I agree!" And with that I gave him a big bear hug and a kiss. By the next day I had the earrings on and they were indeed stunning. We went to the divorce group that night and there were many oohs and awes over the announcement while the women checked out the new earrings.

A week or so went by and I was out shopping for something for the girls when I spotted a beautiful gold man's ring in the jewelry counter at Jordan Marsh. It seemed so unfair that in an engagement the woman got a gift as a promise to the future but the man got nothing. I had the clerk behind the counter take the man's ring out of the case. It was a large, very plain, almost modern looking brushed gold ring with a polished brown stone. I asked her what the stone was and she said it was a Sardonyx, Sy's birth stone for the month of August. Perfect! It was perfect. It was pricey but I didn't care, it was for Sy.

The following weekend the girls were busy in their play and I brought out the ring in its velvet box. He opened the box and said nothing for a moment. "Honey, this is a beautiful ring. You didn't have to get anything for me," he said. Sy put the ring on and it fit. I thought it looked gorgeous on his hand—so masculine, yet tasteful. But there was something about his response that was off.

At one point during the next week I asked out of the blue, "What's wrong with the ring?"

"Nothing is wrong with the ring. Boy, you don't miss a trick," he said.

"I could read your facial expression when I gave it to you and there was something wrong," I said.

"No, there is nothing wrong with the ring. It's that I don't wear any ring but my wedding band. I don't know why, I just don't."

I was crushed and he could see that.

"I tell you what. It is such a lovely ring and the sentiment is so dear, I will wear it whenever we go out to a fine restaurant to eat or go to a special event. Will that help?" he asked.

It did help and he was true to what he said. He didn't wear it often, but he did wear it for all special occasions. And it now sits in his jewelry box, waiting for his youngest grandson to become twenty-one or graduate from high school, whichever seems appropriate. Since it is Robbie's birthstone also, I hope he, too, will wear it for special occasions.

MEETING CUSTARD

Chapter Eight

One of the dates that I didn't include in the dating section was still very important to our relationship. It was a cold late fall evening and Sy had asked if we could hire my baby sitter to sit with both families of girls in my Grows Town home. We called Sharon and she said she could sit especially if May would not be part of the group. We agreed. This way we could have a quiet time together at Sy's home in Nerme almost like married people. He would cook the dinner and then we would both clean up. After the dishes were done he asked if I'd like a tour of his home since he especially wanted to show me where he had closed off a door to create a larger area for book shelves. Of course I agreed to the tour. He proudly presented his carpentry skills and I was impressed by his handiwork.

His living room was set up like a library with bookshelves lining one whole side of the room. He showed me various books and asked if I'd read any of them. I told him that I hadn't and had to confess that I wasn't really a reader since I read very slowly and for content so, I mostly read psychology and self-help books. Okay, did I like poetry? Indeed I did. He pulled off his selves an anthology of poems and opened to one that he loved—Ogden Nash's "Custard the Cowardly Dragon."

As he read I heard about Belinda, a little girl, living in a little white house with a black kitten, a little gray mouse, a yellow dog, a red wagon, and a special, oh, so special, little pet dragon. The poem went on to describe Custard as a dragon with big sharp teeth, spikes on top of his head and scales underneath his belly. His mouth was as big as a fireplace, his nose was the chimney, and last but not least, he had daggers on his toes.

Custard's playmates teased him and disparaged him, but one day there was a disturbance in the playroom. They all heard a nasty sound coming from the window. Belinda gasped Ooh! Then it happened! A pirate was actually climbing in their window. While her animal friends scattered far and wide, Belinda cried, Help! Help! The pirate took one look at Custard and gulped some fortitude from his pocket flagon. He even fired two bullets but they missed their target, and next thing you knew, Custard gobbled up the dastardly pirate, gobbled him up by every bit. Belinda now is as brave as can be because she owns her very own, personal, very special, dragon. The animals are most respectful of Custard, but in spite of it all, Custard keeps crying for a nice safe cave.

As Sy read this poem, I heard how Sy would be my protector against any invading force and for that service he only wanted a "warm safe cave." I thought to myself that is the one thing that I can give this man and his girls. My mission was set. Our partnership sealed.

Often at Christmas time there would be a package under the Christmas tree for Custard and the girls soon learned that it was for Sy. Gradually, there were also packages for Lady Custard. Even today, sometimes, the girls will refer to one or the other of us with these names. And as I write this now, I am realizing that the first home we owned in the Green Trees section of Nerme was colored the same color as Custard. I guess that is why we never re-stained the Ugly Green House.

At Sy's memorial service I read this poem in its poetic form and Rev. John spoke about how Sy was always there, if necessary, to eat any pirate that crossed my path for all of our thirty-five years of marriage.

Because of the copy right laws, I have used here, the version of the poem that I heard that day, but if you would like to read the original, I believe you can still find it in a children's version at Amazon.com.

FIRST THANKSGIVING AND CHRISTMAS

Chapter Nine

I had always spent Thanksgiving with my mother and father in Shakerton, Massachusetts, dragging Harvard and the children with me. So I was hoping that Sy and his girls would be willing to do the same. I don't remember much about that first Thanksgiving in Shakerton except how happy I was, how warm it was in my mother's home, and how great the table looked with so many faces and little squirming bodies seated around the turkey feast. My Aunt Agnes, my father's cousin, was there and added her boisterous personality to the festivities along with her Fanny Farmer's mint candies. Now, I marvel at how my mother who had lost my father four months before was able to prepare all the food, the home made candies, the vegetables, the turkey and the desserts. We arrived the night before and she set the girls to stuffing dates, which Sy's children had never even seen done before. Early Thanksgiving morning Kitty, the third one down, was up and in the kitchen to help her Gramma with the preparations. My mother had always created the Thanksgiving dinner when my father was alive, but now, with my having lost Sy a week before Thanksgiving last year, I am in awe at her fortitude and caring. If asked, she would say, "But that's what makes a holiday for me, having all of my family here under one roof."

It was after Thanksgiving that Grampa Joe brought us the news that Gramma Bootsie was ill, in fact she was very sick with asbestos related cancer. She was such a trooper at Halloween that none of us were aware of the situation. The authorities decided that she had contracted the cancer at her work place but it was too late by the time it was diagnosed to do anything to save her. Sy went to visit her at her home and later in the hospital. I asked if I could go and Sy was surprised and relieved that I wanted to accompany him. She had been such a part of the girl's growing up and I recognized that these grandparents had often taken care of the girls when Sy felt he couldn't leave them alone with their mother.

Bootsie was very feeble by the time I got there but she reached out and took my hand and squeezed it. "I'm so glad you are going to be a part of Sy and the girl's lives. You are such a blessing to us." I could not hold back the tears, not so much for myself but for Sy, Joe, and the girls. She passed away before Christmas. When Grampa Joe came to mourn with us he brought some of her effects from the hospital. There were two plastic pill cups among the things and I still have one left, today. I believe it is her way of looking in on me these thirty-seven years later.

The funeral is vague in my mind, now, but I was saddened that Bootsie's daughter, Sy's soon to be ex-wife, couldn't sit through the service. As an alcoholic who had issues with her mother, I expect there were too many unfinished memories for her to handle. She wandered in the vestibule of the funeral home as I sat with Sy and their daughters, along with my girls through the service.

Christmas time in my home was always Christmas morning. Harvard, as the minister, had not wanted the girls to associate Santa Claus with Christmas so we had talked about Saint Nicolas's works of charity and gifts in the shoes. Sy's girls couldn't wrap their heads around shoes instead of stockings. I think it was stockings by the next year. That first year Sy picked up a tree at a gas station and brought it home to my Grows Town home to be decorated for Christmas. I can't remember, but I think Sy and I did the decorating that year. The extended family was invited—that included Gramma Celia, Grampa Joe, my younger, still single, brother Coppy, or Copeland, as he has been called of late, and my mother.

Sy's children had always been allowed one gift on Christmas Eve so my girls were delighted with the change in plan and angled for the biggest gift. Next morning after the shoe/stockings and breakfast we gathered around the Christmas tree for the big gifts. After we were assembled in my open living room, Sy took the position my father had always held of picking out the gifts and handing them to their designated owner. My girls had been taught to wait as each person unwrapped his or her gift. Sy's girls tore into their packages so there was some negotiating of how things were going to be done moving forward.

At some point in the festivities, Grampa Joe began to cry and shouted out that he couldn't go on this way without Bootsie. The family was stunned and it was my mother who said the calming words about how hard it was to move forward alone, but that it would get better in time. The whole incident made a great impression on all the girls and they still mention it to this day at Christmas time. Having lost Sy last year just before the holidays, I can better empathize with Joe's emotions.

After Gramma Bootsie's will was probated, Sy was informed that there was an inheritance from her to him with a stipulation. It was a nice sum of money, some of which Sy gave back to Grampa Joe. She stated that she wanted a portion of the money used to buy something that the whole family could share and thereby remember her and her love for her grandchildren—all of them. We talked back and forth and decided to have two tiffany hanging lamps designed to hang in our home; one over the dining room table and one in another room in the house. I believe she watches us from these vantage points on many days. The lamps have both moved with us from house to house over the last thirty-five years and the surprising thing is there has always been the perfect spot for each of them.

TO FIND A HOUSE

Chapter Ten

Christmas was over and we were becoming more and more committed to one another so now we needed a house for our five girls, especially a house that might have enough bedrooms for all.

There was a section of Nerme that I had come to years before as part of a woman's group and I loved the area; in fact, I had told several people that if I ever moved from Grows Town I wanted to live in the Green Trees part of Nerme.

We contacted a realtor and told him that we needed at least five bedrooms. He explained that that would be a tall order to fill, but he would show us what he had. Two of the houses didn't even make it onto the list. He showed us a Dutch Colonial in Comfortville and, when we said we didn't want to live in Comfortville, he commented that he had the same house, a little larger and modified a bit, in Nerme. In fact he had two in the same area that were for sale—new and never lived in before. We followed him to the location and found they were in the lower end of the Green Tree section, the area where I said I wanted to live.

Both of the houses sat up on a rise with other smaller houses all encircled by a road that ran at the base of that rise. Each one looked impressive. One was more modern in style and we turned that one down quickly. The second was the Dutch Colonial, more traditional and stained an ugly green. You could see from the outside that it might be large enough, but to live the rest of our lives with that color! Sy said he could re-stain it if that was what we chose. We went inside and we both fell in love. The rooms were large with windows almost floor to ceiling. There was a large master bedroom with on-suite and a large walk-in closet with a window. The other bedrooms were large as well, the only problem seemed that the two youngest girls would have to share a room—but they were young, they could adjust.

The living room was back to front and the dining room on the opposite side of the main door had a picture window looking out onto the sloping front lawn encircling a cluster of trees. We asked the price and winced. Sy told the realtor that we liked the place but would have to think about it. We were told that it would be selling quickly so we'd better think about putting in an offer. I could hardly fall asleep that night as I mulled over in my mind where we were going to come up with $83,000.00 dollars. Next day had to have been a Sunday and Sy and I sat contemplating how we were going to pull off this feat. Finally I said, "We have the money from my divorce settlement."

"You would use it for this purpose?" Sy asked. "It is your money. You worked and earned it over the years."

"Of course I would use it for this purpose. It is our future and the future of the girls." And so it was decided that a part of that sum of money would go to buy a new red Chevrolet van that could transport all of us at one time and the rest would be the down payment on our house in the Green Tree section of Nerme.

As with all house purchases, there were papers to gather, trips to the bank, meetings with the lawyers, and more papers to sign, but eventually the Ugly Green House became ours.

I then began the planning of where things would go. Sy convinced me that our old things with their painful memories could be donated and we could purchase some new pieces especially for the living room. I chose a medium green velvet love seat and he chose a cream and blue striped sofa with a fine line of pink flowers next to the blue. We purchased a desk-like table where the fish tank would sit in the front window. And would you believe, I have my computer sitting on that same desk as I write these memories?

Sy, brave soul that he was, accompanied me to a fabric outlet store where we chose the fabric for the living room curtains. Having sewn since I was ten, making curtains for a living room didn't daunt me. I'm not sure

I felt the same way after they were done. I did love that fabric, and kept a remnant for many years.

There was still some finishing work to do in the living room, so we did not move in for some time, besides, there were two other houses to sell and pack. We actually moved into the ugly green house on Valentine's Day in 1978, but that is grist for a later story.

MOVING DAY

Chapter Eleven

Christmas vacation from school found Sy and I each encouraging our youngsters to start packing their things as we began the immense job of packing up two houses and preparing them to be sold. The details on this part of the job are sketchy to me now. I remember my house was sold to a maiden lady who needed the lower area of the house for her aging parents. She seemed pleasant and I was relieved at who was buying my house.

I don't remember the details of the preparation and sale of Sy's house, probably because he was always inclined to take care of business without much comment or complaining. I do remember his looking at the few remaining plants I had on the lower level of my house, scraggly plants raised by a single mother who was too busy to even breathe at times, and asking, "So what are we supposed to do with these?" The emphasis was on these, like how about we throw them all away. I wasn't going along with the plan and he only looked vexed for a couple of seconds.

We closed the sale of both houses and moved the contents of both houses on that same day. You can believe it took all day long to do this. I remember that we used the same moving crew for both houses and Sy had it pretty well figured out as to which house contents would be packed into the truck first, because of what items we would need to unpack first to start a new life in Nerme.

Because the children were in different schools—Grows Town and Nerme--we decided the best plan was to move just before the February school vacation and be married at the end of that week so that my mother would have an easier job of caring for the children while they were attending school. Mother Nature thought it was a marvelous plan and sent the blizzard of 1978 three days before we were scheduled to move. That left Sy snow bound on one side of the Cold Star Bridge in Whaling City and I snow bound on the other side of the bridge. I couldn't get the car out to do errands and the girls were still pretty small to be shoveling that kind of snow. If you possibly remember, Governor Grasso closed the roads during that storm. And worse yet, Sy and I couldn't get to see or console each other. I remember getting out there with my snow shovel and grumbling to myself that Sy and I were now separated by this immense snow storm--unfair. When I was about two thirds of the way done with the long driveway at my house, two boys came along and asked, "Do you need any help with this driveway, Ma'am?" I answered "I sure do and thank you very much!" You can believe I paid them more than the usual.

The actual moving day was on Valentine's Day—how appropriate. Fortunately it was mild and sunny and very long. It was about 7:00 o'clock in the evening when two exhausted moving men had a mattress on their shoulders, and standing at the base of the front stairs at the Ugly Green House in Nerme, they asked me, "So where do you want us to put this mattress, Ma'am?" I laugh now at my response, "I don't know. It isn't my mattress!" They didn't think it was so funny and I quickly came up with a destination. About then, we were all punch drunk with exhaustion. Supper was pizza on paper plates, I think in the dining room, because we had moved my maple dining room set from Grows Town.

We finally got the girl's beds set up, put together, and the sheets and blankets on but we had decided that we did not want to sleep in a bed that had been shared with an ex-spouse so we had ordered a beautiful Van Horn canopy bed for the master bed room from the Marvel Barn in Marvel, Connecticut. That night we had the lovely lace topper and the mattress but not the bed frame. We started life at the Ugly Green House sleeping on a firm mattress on the floor. We were so exhausted that no one could have fallen out of bed, anyway.

MARCHING TOWARD A WEDDING

Chapter Twelve

We knew early on there would be a wedding, but now came the discussion of what kind of a wedding. Both of us had had the traditional wedding before; mine with all the flowers and dresses and photographs. His was smaller, according to the existing pictures, and I'm not sure if it was a church wedding or not. Family was there, that was certain. So now what was it that would be right for us? We decided that we wanted no frills, no church, just family and a very few friends, mostly those from our divorce group. If the wedding wasn't to be in a church then where should it be held? Silly question; it should be in the home where we met, and besides being a therapist David Eaton was an ordained minister. It was decided we would be married in street clothes in front of David and Jodie's fireplace in their front room in Olbrooke, Connecticut. The date was set for February 25, 1978.

I did want a special dress even though it was to be street length. I don't remember where I shopped, but I do remember that it was a little brown dress in a soft jersey-like material with cream and bright orange accents on the collar and an orange scarf tied and tucked in at the throat. When my daughters clear my clothes for the Salvation Army they will find the little brown dress at the back of all the others. I do remember that it was the first dress I tried on and I was disappointed that I'd found it so quickly. But, after trying others, it was the little brown dress that was right. The shoes went the same way—cream, strappy sandals with a small heel.

When it was Sy's turn for new clothes he wanted me to go with him. He was one of the few men I know who actually liked to shop. We found a wool tweed sport jacket in medium blue, with navy and cream slubs in the weave. He looked so handsome, his curly brown hair and sideburns recently trimmed. He was certainly a prize of a man

Next we needed to find, or have made, our wedding rings. We decided that we wanted rings fashioned to symbolize the fact that this was not a first marriage and there were influences from other people being woven into this marriage. Sy had heard of a new jeweler working in Mystand, Connecticut, so we took an afternoon off and went to find Daniel and Co. He was just starting out in his business and was working out of the old factory on a side street. We parked the car on the street, but Sy didn't make a move to get out. I looked at him because his expression had changed from the easy conversation we had been having as we drove into town.

"What's wrong I asked? Don't you want to get married?"

He looked flustered for a moment and then said, "I have something to tell you before we go in and you may not want to go ahead with this marriage once you know."

My heart sank, but I'd rather he be truthful than hide something until after the wedding. So, I said, "Tell me. I can't believe it is terrible enough to call off a wedding." He started into his confession and I was stunned. I sat silent trying to absorb what he was saying and weighing its impact on our marriage. When finished, he waited as if holding his breathe.

"Because you are telling me and taking the risk that I might back away," I said, "I feel I can trust you moving forward. So let's go get our rings!" His breathing returned to normal and he leaned over, took me in his arms, and kissed me.

I can still remember looking at the beautiful silver jewelry and crystal goblets on the shelves in the new store while rolling over in my mind if this was the right thing to be doing--but it couldn't be any other way. I could not live without this man. By the time Daniel was done with the customer in front of us, I was settled and we talked to him about our rings. He heard and understood our wish to have wide gold bands made of strands of gold symbolizing the other people in our lives. He fashioned the most beautiful wide gold bands consisting of four interwoven strands of gold. When we came back to pick them up, they fit perfectly.

Since Sy died a year ago in November, I have just finished wearing his ring on a gold chain around my neck to symbolize the formal year of mourning, but more so to have some part of him still close to my heart. His confession will go with me to my grave. We both made the right decisions.

The next step was to get the wedding license. We were surprised to find there was no blood test necessary as there had been with a first marriage and that the license had to be taken out in the town where we would be married. It took a bit to find the right location in Olebrooke but the license was applied for and given.

Flowers were not so much of an issue. In fact, I wasn't planning on any, but Sy said that was something he wanted to give me. I settled on white daisy, a flower from my childhood, and something that we could get in the middle of the winter. So, when the day came I stood in front of David's fireplace in my brown dress, holding a bunch of white daisies. (For anyone who is interested, the painting that always hangs in the front hall of my home is a picture of a field of daises done by a local artist. Since the flowers wouldn't keep, the picture represents my daisies.)

The music was my domain and I asked Irene, the woman who was the lead soprano in the Grows Town Congregational Church that my girls and I had just left, if she could sing without accompaniment for us. She agreed and sang the song that had become our love song, "Morning Has Broken" made popular by Kat Stevens. She also sang "The Twenty Third Psalm—the Lord is my Shepherd." I am hoping that my girls remember these are two of the songs I want when it is my time to join Sy, along with "The Ode to Joy" from Beethoven's 9th Symphony.

And now we come to the cake. I said I could make one and Sy suggested we just bring one in from Milton's bakery. I noticed the girls looked crestfallen and asked what was wrong. "We were going to make your cake! Kitty already has picked out a recipe!" And so it was decided. They struggled and as you could expect, since this was a big occasion, the cake didn't come out just the way they wanted. I had to remind Kitty that I'd made her a birthday cake when she was about seven and the whole center stayed in the pan. At the time she looked at the improbable cake and said, "Don't worry, Mummy. Put frosting in the middle and it will taste just as good." Their cake tasted wonderful when Sy gave me a piece, but better than that is the dear memory that our girls cared enough to make our wedding cake.

THE WEEK OF THE WEDDING

Chapter Thirteen

Somewhere before our wedding we had already started the ritual of excusing the girls from the dining room as soon as we were all done with our evening meal. This was our "coffee time" and the girls' job was to clear the table and fill the dishwasher. I would finish the pots and pans later. We used this time to catch up with each other, our day's events, and to strategize about any issues that had or we could see would be coming up with the girls, especially points of discipline.

It had to have been early in that week before our wedding when I confessed to Sy that I sometimes needed to get away from it all, maybe even him. I had been alone now for well over a year and I wasn't sure how that need would play out. He was silent for a moment and then he grabbed my hand, "Come!" he commanded as he got up. He pulled me out the French doors of the dining room and up the staircase heading towards I didn't know where. He rounded the corner at the top of the stairs and pulled me into our bedroom. Without speaking he opened the door to our walk-in closet. I looked at him in question. "It has a window and I'll put a chair in there for you. Will that do?" he asked. I was so taken aback at how perfect it was and how well he understood what I was saying that all I could do was laugh. Would you believe, I never had to use it although the chair was there for me!

The girls were all home from school on vacation and Sy was still at work, always one to work up until the last minute. As the week wore on, the ranker and excitement grew among the girls. The fights and disagreements mounted and I couldn't seem to intervene in any meaningful way. Nobody paid attention, and what's more, they didn't seem to care what I thought. I couldn't believe that these lovely girls of the last few months had become monsters. On Wednesday I locked myself in the downstairs bathroom and cried because I didn't think I was going to be able to carry this off--to parent these tiny tyrants!!

After the honeymoon, I later found out my mother and the fill-in baby sitter had much the same feeling and thoughts, but that is a later story.

My mother had volunteered--or maybe was coerced--I'm not sure which, into coming to stay with our darlings for the first half of the week that followed the wedding, which would be our honeymoon. What to do for the other half of the week? As is so often true, someone at church suggested one of the widow women who baby sat for children associated with the Nerme Family Church. I forget her name at the moment--Oh, yes, Millie Francis. She was a lovely older lady. We interviewed her and thought she would be a great fill in. Come to find out she was used to taking care of small children, not ones that were creeping toward adolescence. They gave her a run for her money, but, thankfully, we didn't know anything about that until after we got back from the honeymoon.

The RSVP's were coming in from our divorce group and from our families. It seemed that several of the people from the group would be there along with my sister who made the long trip down from Vermont alone, and my younger brother who came in from New York State. My mother planned to drive down from Massachusetts and stay through the first part of the next week. The 'encroaching lady' (see, I still can't remember her name) called, identified herself, and I didn't recognize the name. I responded, "Who?" She repeated the name again and I still didn't get it. "Who is calling?" I asked her. Finally she said, "It doesn't really matter. I can't come to the wedding, anyhow!" I'm sorry to have to admit that even my unconscious feelings play tricks with my mind.

The third thing that seemed to surface that week was that the two youngest girls, Felicia and Annie, the 'his 'n her twins,' (both being the same age but of different lineage) were having trouble sharing one big bedroom. Unfortunately, we were too focused on getting this wedding done to really hear them clearly. Not getting enough sleep for each of them may have been adding to the chaos. Blended families? We were about to take off on the long and painstaking adventure which ultimately seemed to turn out reasonably well. We did eventually become a true blended family.

THE WEDDING AND AFTERMATH

Chapter Fourteen

February 25, 1978, dawned bright, crisp, and cold. It seemed surreal to roll off of one side of a mattress resting on the cold master bedroom floor while my soon to be spouse rolled off of the other side. This was the room that would be the container for our personal love for the--who knows--how many future years. We both sat on the cold wooden floor for a moment looking at each other and he must have been having the same thoughts because we both giggled. Who knew what would lie ahead for the two of us? Joy, disaster, fights, harmony or the deep and sustaining love, laced with laughter that we did experience with the years. Then it was off to get washed up and ready for the day and the multitude of things that had to be done before we got to our 2:00 o'clock afternoon wedding.

The guests were gathering at David and Jodie's house. We had gone to pick up Gramma Celia in Whaling City and were surprised to see people already at David's house when we arrived. My sister, PollyAnne, was there from Vermont and my younger brother, Coppy, from New York State, arrived just before the service started. My mother was already there since she was going to be staying at our home in Nerme with the girls. Grampa Joe had driven himself.

Gramma Celia leaned forward in the car and tapped me on the shoulder. "I need a moment of your time before the service starts," she said. It sounded very formal. When we went into the pastor's house I motioned to Celia to follow me into Jodie's kitchen. "It's nothing great, but I wanted you to have this. You know the something old, something new, borrowed, and blue. This is the something old." With that she pulled out of her hand bag a handkerchief, and as she opened it for me to peek inside, there was an exquisite, large, salmon and cream colored cameo wrapped in silver leaf work that could only have been carved years ago in Italy. "This is yours and I want you to wear this today. It is very important to me." She didn't have to tell me that this was a piece of jewelry that her past husband, Leo, had given her early in their marriage. You could feel the love that she was giving to me as she released the cameo and antique chain into my hands. Being also of practical mind, I thought, this dress has a shirt collar on it and there is no way I can wear a cameo and have it show. Then I realized that I could use the pin part to anchor the orange scarf to the lapel of the dress and it would look like it had been planned. When you look at the pictures you can see the cameo is there and I believe Leo was also. What did I say about the wedding rings having many strands of gold?!

With high celebrations like this, one remembers snap shots rather than a continuous slide show. I remember standing in front of Rev. David Eaton who had his back to their living room fireplace. Sy was standing beside me and I felt so calm and grounded in my little brown dress and strappy sandals. Sy looked confident, too, and handsome in his blue tweed jacket and darker slacks. I think we both were so sure that we were designed to be together that there were no last minute jitters. The surprise was that David filled up with tears as he led us through our vows—a testament to the years he had spent with both of us building a relationship and helping us grow in strength, able to make this kind of a commitment, knowing that it would indeed work out as we dreamed.

JessieMay and Sy's Wedding Ceremony
Jessie, Rev. David Eaton, and Sy

    The musical pieces sung as solos were lovely and the girls lined up on Jodie and David's couch (the one I sat on as I saw Sy for the first time) with the usual pushing and positioning for the best view. I felt we were so surrounded by good wishes and the expectation that this marriage would go the distance--until death do us part.

    When the service was over, Jodie brought out the cake that the girls had made and handed over her special knife and cake server for us to cut the cake. At my first wedding I remember fearing that Harvard, being a mischief maker, might shove the cake down my throat but with this little wedding I knew my new husband would be as loving and gracious to me as he had been in everything else we had encountered so far. And indeed what few pictures we have illustrate that spirit between us. The cake was delicious!

The Wedding Cake
Jessie Feeding Sy a Piece of the Wedding Cake Made by Their Daughters

One of the women from our divorce group presented us with a scroll on which she had drawn in beautiful manuscript the whole poem of "Custard the Cowardly Dragon." That piece hung in our front hall for many years. There were other gifts, mostly money which we certainly needed at that point.

When all the festivities were done, we gathered up our coats and went outside to make our way to the red van which was packed and ready to head toward Bunker City and our honeymoon get away. The air was crystal clear while the sky was so blue and so bright I remember thinking the Gods are certainly blessing this union. Our guests threw rice as we got into the van, giving us the feeling of a rain shower. I think it was the girls' idea and I'm not sure why they did it since we planned to have no more children, but they didn't know that yet. We drove away into an unknown future, I still holding my white daisies.

The trip north was leisurely and delightful as we chatted, sharing things about the wedding and dreaming about the future. It was perhaps the first time since we had met that there was no pressure of children or the next thing that needed to be accomplished. Sy had made arrangements for a room at the Hartwell Jones's Hotel in Kenneth Square. We pulled up to this somewhat seedy two story hotel and my heart dropped. At this point I need to give you back story for you to understand my dismay.

When Harvard and I were married in 1962, he had been very busy, as most ministers are right before Christmas, and so set his best man to making the reservations for our first night of marriage. His best man, a New York City gentleman, knew nothing about Massachusetts, and made a reservation at the Stonebridge Village Inn, in central Massachusetts. Once married, Harvard and I drove through the remnants of an ice storm to our reservation at the Inn. The woman gave us our keys and pointed us toward the giant dance hall that was rocking with a Christmas office party and told us to take the stairs up to our room. When we arrived we had twin beds in a tiny room, as I said, just above the revelers. Harvard lost his temper—had a hissy fit, as my girls later termed them--at the bell hop, at me, later at the receptionist and literally dragged his suitcase, leaving me to drag mine, back through the ice coated parking lot. We stayed at a motel down the road.

Back to the Bunker City story: I'm looking at the outside of the hotel and beginning to wonder if this is a sign, a warning as the last had been, of the life to come. We got our room keys and went up to our second story room. There was a double bed, dirty and lumpy, the wallpaper was dingy and the curtains drooped. I sat down on the side of the bed; my bunch of daisies still clutched in my hands, and fought back the tears. Sy went to the radio—as I later learned he always did when we went to a hotel—and fiddled with the dial. The next thing I heard was a sweet voice singing "Morning Has Broken," --our wedding song!

I looked at him and asked, "Did you pay room service to play that song when we got here?"

"No, Honey, it just came on when I moved the dials."

A Bird and the Dragon: Their Love Story

All the fear left me. Whether Sy had programed it or God looked down and knew I needed reassurance, I was listening to our beautiful love song. Dinner was horrible and breakfast worse.

At the end of breakfast Sy said, "Let's go over to the Sherman Hotel and talk to one of the house maids. Maybe she will let us look at a room." We did, and she did, and we moved into the Sherman Hotel. Somehow they found out we were newly married and we had the best of everything.

There were meals out and breakfasts in and time to just be with each other. One event that still lingers is the trip to the symphony at Symphony Hall. Sy made reservations for the concert, and then, at the suggestion of David and Jodie, we had reservations at the Budapest Room for dinner. If you could remember, you would know that Bunker City was blanketed in about three feet or more of snow in the winter of 1978. The cars had pompoms or ribbons or some sort of marker on their radio antennas so that one could pull out of a side street onto the main roads without being struck.

It had started to snow again, a lazy, fluffy snow and I questioned the wisdom in going, but Sy said not to worry we'd just hail a cab. We were driven to the Budapest Room and entered a foreign world of marble and ornate woodwork. I don't remember dinner clearly except that it was delicious and moderate in size. Then there was my usual trip to the ladies room. When I came back Sy said I could hardly contain myself. "You should see the ladies room! Marble everywhere in tones of green and more tiles in maroons and wood and flowers and gold faucets! I've never seen anything so lovely!"

In Sy's special way he said, "I sounds like the ladies room is more of a hit than the restaurant." I guess, in terms of those things that stick in our minds, it was.

We came out from the restaurant and found the cabs wheeling and turning, jostling in the snow to get their next fare. All the cabs were filled, and finally, a single woman tapped on the window and then opened the door. "Where are you going?" she called.

"To the symphony," Sy replied.

"Climb in!" she offered. "It is just I, and I'm going right by Symphony Hall." We got in and this lovely lady quickly found out that we were on our honeymoon. She wished us well and waved us off at the entrance to the hall. --Funny how a chance, momentary meeting, can stick with you for thirty-six, almost thirty-seven years.

Another adventure was the walk home. It was still snowing lightly and we decided to walk. Our route took us along the side of one of the large public buildings in Bunker City. At that time there was a park-like area to the side of the building and large pillars creating a portico with a lighted overhang. The spot lights shone out onto the darkened park. As we walked past the pillars the snow blew from the roof, swirling, turning and uplifting, and then twisting to settle on whatever was below. We were covered in a dusting of light snow when we got to the hotel. Somehow the light beams shining through the snow were simply magical and I will always remember that night.

What a fitting start to an equally memorable union!

DRATS! REENTRY!

Chapter Fifteen

We arrived home most likely on Sunday afternoon to be greeted by our child care person; Millie Francis, who I think, may have had her coat on ready to leave. As I said, my mother had the first shift in the week and Millie the last. Two of the three toilets weren't working and she didn't know whom to call. Although she didn't really say so, the girls had given her a merry chase being anything but cooperative and she couldn't wait to be free. We thanked her profusely and paid her for her time. I think Sy drove her home.

Now the girls' side of the story is different. Ms. Francis wouldn't let them do anything. She talked down to them. She didn't get the toilet fixed and she was just out of touch! Sy called the plumber and the work of our marriage began. Laundry!! Mountains of it! Even though Cora was fourteen by now and had been supervising her father's home for years, somehow no laundry got done after my mother left.

My girls, Happy and Kitty, had joined their step-sisters in the Nerme Town school system and did not like their new school very much. Apparently they were getting the "new kid" treatment and being teased about their names. Happy came to us some time after we got home and announced that she no longer wanted to be called Happy as she was no longer happy. She had been called Happy since toddlerhood because of her disposition and given name, but now she wanted us to use her real name of Felicia. When I went to my mother with the same request --to no longer be Birdie, as my grandmother had nicknamed me, my mother smiled and said, "Well, you'll always be Birdie to me!" With Gramma Sands that was the end of the subject and she never honored my request. Sy had heard the story and my hurt. He looked at Happy and said, "Then you will be Felicia from now on."

One bright note on re-entry was that the wedding bed we had ordered made for our master bedroom had arrived while we were gone and my mother had made it up with the sheets and blankets that she could find. The canopy was not on because she said she looked at the pile of fishnet (her words) and couldn't figure out how to get it up there, let alone straight. And for my mother, if you couldn't get it on straight, best not even try.

One event I left out of our honeymoon story was the fact that in walking by Filene's department store we saw bed sheets on display in the front windows. We both fell in love with their pattern, expensive as they were, and I wanted them so badly that we went in to buy a souvenir of our honeymoon trip. They didn't have any in the store. They had sold out. We pleaded. We were on our honeymoon and these were to be a memento of the week! Finally, they called around to their outlying stores and sent us to a store outside of Bunker City. We made a day trip of it and when we got there they had the sheets, but no pillow cases. Those they would order and ship. Half satisfied, we stopped and had a hamburger and enjoyed whichever town we were in at that time.

Back home, I think it must have been the next day or on the next weekend, I stripped off the bedding my mother had provided and put on our new sheets, and by now, the pillow cases. Luxury! Luxury! I think the last fragments of those sheets were sold with the under-bed baskets and different bedstead when we left Nerme Village, a year and a half ago. I really loved those sheets so much I had used them to make dust covers for the under-bed baskets. By then, the sheets were too frail to be used in any other way.

It is funny the memories that stay with you, but I can still feel the headboard of that bed, stained in a red-based mahogany stain on pine. The headboard was one piece and had been cut right through a giant knot so all of the holes and crevasses showed. Many a time when I was contemplating something instead of sleeping, I would reach up and run my hands over that knot since it was positioned on my side of the bed. Even today, I still miss that four poster bed.

Not too long after we returned, Felicia and Annie came to us to explain that they could not get along with each other in bunk beds in one room. Annie was neat by nature and Felicia just the opposite. Felicia complained that any idea she had, Annie wanted to copy. Could they please have their big room split in half? Since we had anticipated that this might be the outcome Sy called in my old carpenter and together they drew up plans to cut the room in half, giving each girl windows and a closet. When the mission was accomplished they seemed to feel more secure in this new family.

Somewhere in that time frame, the girls began to set up their alliances. Felicia and Elizabeth--who also began to use her given name--had always been close in Grows Town, and when May went to live with her father for the year, they became even closer. In this new environment Felicia was drawn to the oldest sister Cora. Elizabeth felt left out and became a loner, and Annie, who had always fended for herself, still went outside the home to make friends. Today the alliances seem to rotate.

The stories from here on will be filled with bits and pieces of memories, not necessarily in order, because, in all honesty, chaos entered our lives once we were married and back in Nerme as "the parents." I have always wondered why we were called that, but watching Felicia and Joseph who were married last December 28, 2013, build their blended family, it becomes clear that there is no better word in our vocabulary that includes the parental role of the step-parent.

And while I'm on names, Felicia came to me a couple of years into our new marriage and said, "Why does Sy call all of us girls 'Boops'?"

I thought for a minute and said, "Because at that moment in time he can't remember who he is talking to so he uses a pet name like 'Boops' for all of you. It means no disrespect."

She responded with, "Oh, okay. I just wondered."

THE SHOE BOX

Chapter Sixteen

It had to have been early in April of that first year of marriage. Sy came home from the office and during our coffee time he said to me, "I've gotten orders to go out on one of the submarines to test some of the things we have been developing." My heart sank, but I tried not to show it. It would be the first time we had been apart since our marriage and I would be in charge of the girls by myself. I was also running around in my head the stories he'd told me about what he had found in the home after coming back in the past from testing runs. 'No, this time we women can hold it together for him,' I thought, but I said, "I will miss you." He reached out to hold my hand and responded, "I'll miss you, too."

We went on to discuss other topics and not much more was said about the testing run. As the days crept closer I kept going from, 'I can do this,' to 'I can't manage these girls alone,' and finally back to, 'Just get your big girl pants on and do it!'

The day arrived. Sy had packed his personal bag and the few other things he would need and it was understood I would drive him to the pier. We talked about whatever on the trip to the ship. I'm sure he gave me last-minute instructions in case something went wrong for that was his way. I pulled the car up a short distance from the ship and we sat for a moment in silence then he said, "Well, I guess this is it." With that he got his things from the back seat and stepped out of the car. He came around to the driver's side and leaned in to give me one more parting kiss. He also slipped a piece of white note paper into my hand.

When I said, "What's this?"

He sort of nodded and said, "You can open it when you get home." One more kiss and I started the engine. He pulled away, turned, and started in his typical gait, heels somewhat together and toes slightly pointed toward the side, to walk toward the ship. I was in an 'I can do this' frame of mind and turned the car around and started to pull out of the parking area. Suddenly I couldn't breathe! I couldn't get air! It was as if some force was sucking everything out of me. Then my rational side kicked in saying, "Now, girly, pull yourself together and drive this thing home."

I did 'pull it together' and with flagging spirits began the run in my mind of what I would have to do first when I got home. I went in and found that the girls were occupied with whatever they were doing so I could turn my attention to the white note paper still clutched in one hand. I opened it and the note said in Sy's characteristic large, confident hand, "Go up to our closet, and on my side, under my hanging clothes you will find a shoe box. It is for you."

I raced up to our closet and flung open the door. Sure enough on his side there was a box shoved in between his shoes. I knelt down and grabbed it. Carefully, I opened the cover and there inside was a Kermit doll in his vivid green garb with bulging happy eyes and a fly eating grin on his face. There was another note. "Kermit is here to help and watch over you while I am away." I just held the stuffed frog and cried.

Kermit gained a position in my kitchen, and sat there supervising the cooking for many years. Over time he became greasy from kitchen vapors and being made of a felt-like fabric and cardboard, he wasn't a candidate for a bath so, finally, with sadness, I put him into my Treasure Box and stowed him away in a closet.

Sy reported that the trip was uneventful and they were able to test what they needed to test. The report was pretty much the same from my side of the aisle.

Now, fast forward to about a year and a half ago. That would be the fall of 2013. Sy and I had moved into our dream home which we had been watching from the distance of our summer cottage while this new house was being built in Forest North, a senior community in Center Town, Connecticut. It had to be in September or the beginning of October. I was unpacking boxes and came across my Treasure Box. I opened it and there was Kermit, still smiling at me even after being shut away for so long. I thought, 'It's time he had a chance to come out and get some fresh air. I have a nick knack shelf in our bathroom and he can sit up there. No one will see that he is still grubby. He can watch us from his new perch.'

Sy died a month later. His last night was spent being very sick under Kermit's watchful eye until I finally said, "We are getting you back to the hospital. And I'm driving you in."

It wasn't until after Sy had passed over and I was back at home cleaning and mourning that I looked up and saw Kermit still smiling down on me. Now how did I know to let him out at this time? Kermit is still there to help me, and watch over me until the day comes when I shall go to join my Sy.

MAY

Chapter Seventeen

I'm not sure where to begin with this chapter--at the beginning or in the middle. The shorter version is probably the better route. Rev. Harvard Lesser and I took May in as a foster child when she was nineteen months old. I was to heal from surgery so that I could bear children and it seemed so long to wait. She arrived at our house as an emergency placement from a home that was being investigated for sexual misconduct. We had never had a child before and we certainly knew little about how to raise her. She was oppositional from the moment I first spoke to her and it has not really faded even as I write. We did adopt her when she was seven years old, believing that if we all knew we would be her 'forever parents,' tensions might ease and our lives change for the better. The adoption didn't change anything. The difference came forty years later. Now I know she has bipolar disorder and is on and off her medications. When off her medications she uses alcohol and drugs.

May is Home on Vacation with Her Mom, Jessie

When I met Sy, May was living with her father in the home that he moved into when I asked for a divorce. His house was located on the back side of the large block in Grows Town that contained the family home. In the spring of the second year when we girls were by ourselves, May began to act up and was lying to me over everything. I was absorbed by the stresses of the divorce and I told her if she lied to me one more time I would do something drastic. She, of course, lied. I went outside and cut a thin branch off the forsythia bush at the side of the house, brought it in, and laid three swats along her leg. There was lots of crying, noise, and ruckus, and then she settled down.

About two weeks later I was standing, about to discipline her for something—and by now she was taller than I--as I started into my rant she snarled, "You can't touch me! Daddy's gonna take you to court! I showed him the bruises you made on my leg!"

Now switching a child is not good discipline and I have learned better methods over the years. The upshot: I realized suddenly I had lost any ability to discipline her in any way. I didn't get much sleep that night. The next morning I called Harvard and explained what May had told me. He listened intently, when I said, "I want to make a proposal. Why don't you take May to live with you for one year? And at the end of the year we can renegotiate who has custody of May." He agreed and at the end of that school calendar, she moved in with her father. She was back at my door within a month complaining that it wasn't anything like home and she wanted to come back and live with us. I pointed out to her that the two of them had agreed to one year.

Now we fast forward to my story. Sy and I were now married. May had spent week-ends with us and the other girls. June was approaching and she would be coming to live with us. The custody issue seemed to have evaporated. We needed to build another bedroom because we knew she would not move into one of the other girls' rooms successfully. The house was designed so that there were ground level windows in the basement at the front of the house. We called our trusty carpenter. He and Sy built a bedroom for May in the front part of the basement.

We now had five girls under one roof. How to keep them occupied and out of mischief? We had little money to spare but decided to take them on a camping trip for two weeks during the summer and some of the rest of the time would be spent with school summer play ground or playing with the neighborhood kids. Our camping trip took us to one of the lakes in New Hampshire where we put up tents and camping equipment and had the use of a lovely beach. I'm sure Sy and I were more focused on each other than we should have been and May tried everything she could think of to torment Cora, her year older step-sister.

None of the girls liked the semi-rustic outside toilet cubbies and Cora came to us in tears one day. While she was using one of them, May was taking wads of wet toilet paper and either throwing them on Cora or decorating the door. Now that is not such a horrible offense, but it was one more in a long string of efforts to disrupt the whole trip. It was the next night when May snuck out of the back side of the tent after lights-out and was gone all night. We found her missing very early in the morning and Sy went hunting for her. He never found her, but when she returned she said she was with one of the boys who maintained the camp grounds.

By the end of August and a continuous round of difficulties with May, Sy and I finally had to agree that she was going to destroy the new family if she stayed with us. Her father did not seem to want to take her back. It looked like boarding school was the only solution. This was not my finest hour but we hunted and found a school here in Connecticut, Breakstone Academy that could take May by the time school opened in September. We didn't warn her of what was going to happen because of the scene she would have created. She only knew at the very last minute where she was going and why. It wasn't until years later that we learned Breakstone was a holding place for the juvenile delinquents in the state who had run out of options.

She lasted at Breakstone until the late spring when we were called in to a faculty interrogation of May and one of the boys. They had been found together in a closet with less than the required amount of clothes on. The boy remained at the school and May was expelled. With the whole summer ahead we were troubled. Then I suggested that all of the children had inherited money through my divorce settlement and Gramma Bootsie's death. We took a small amount from each girl and had a semi in ground pool built in our back yard. The garage being attached to the house as it was formed an L shape, and the pool was tucked into that back corner.

Sy spent the early summer building a deck around the two exposed sides and the required railings to meet town codes. It was a lovely spot and did much to sooth the family situation. By now her father was ready to have May in his home since he had married again. May started high school with them and lasted almost a year with them and then she ran away and her father would not go after her so the police picked her up and she spent some time in juvenile lock up.

From there she came back to us and we enrolled her in Chestnut Academy. This time she did have a chance to visit the school and was somewhat in agreement to go. It was a fine school and she learned a lot academically. Towards the end of her second spring in the Academy, the school called and asked if I had been in a car accident. No, I had not. Had I recently given birth to a little boy who had died? No, I had not. They suggested that we come and bring May home for a psychiatric evaluation.

We found an excellent psychiatrist in Whaling City, and yes, he would see May. She came home and went to therapy for about three weeks. The school called to remind us that May was due to take her finals soon and we needed to find out if she was well enough to go through that process. The doctor said that he felt she was perfectly capable of taking her exams. She was furious, went back to Chestnut, and flunked every exam.

The core family was beginning to blend but if we brought May home to stay she would again try to destroy it with her jealousy and frustration. I believe it was that summer when she would leave the house at night without permission and roam the bars picking up whatever males she could find. One night Sy got up in the middle of the night and checked all the bars, then walked the railroad tracks in town and finally returned home without her. She returned about noon the next day telling us that she had met up with some boys on bicycles and they had spent the night prowling around town.

We asked the psychiatrist for any help or suggestions for our sake and her safety. Shortly, he told us of a school in Pennsylvania that was devoted to guiding children like May who needed a very structured environment while still being taught academically and socially acceptable ways to live in the world. She was accepted and stayed at Devereux Mental Health Facility for Troubled Young People until she was eighteen.

May had matured to the place where the school was planning to put her in a coed dorm and begin teaching her a trade. In Pennsylvania at that time, a child of eighteen was now an independent. She told us she was going to run away from school. Sy and I made the long drive down to the school and sat with May, her advisors, and her therapist whom she had grown to respect. For seven hours we discussed, pleaded, explained, and tried in any way we could to show her the advantage of staying and learning a trade. In desperation I finally said, "If you get up and walk out of that door you will be walking out of my life forever. I'm not kidding!" She took one look at me, got up, walked to the door, waved, and walked out.

I could go on and on about May's life after this. Suffice it to say, it has not been a happy one because she slid into alcohol and drugs and misery. Her sisters fault both Sy and I, mostly me, for not keeping her in the family. But I'm not sure they really understand how different all of our lives would have been if that had happened.

It wasn't until a few years ago that May went to a clinic in the area of Indiana where she now lives and was diagnosed with Bipolar Depression. As a therapist I could kick myself that I didn't recognize it, but back when she was a child nobody knew much about the disorder or how to treat and medicate a child. As a child she was given Ritalin to relieve the ADHD symptoms. We were told that if it made no changes in her behavior she did not have ADHD. When she took it nothing changed. So the subject was dropped. At that point in my life I was not yet trained as a therapist so didn't continue to ask questions. Even if I had known, she might well have still floundered. Back then they didn't know how to medicate a child with Bipolar Depression and in many communities still don't.

You may be asking why I spend a whole chapter on one of the children in the family and I can only say that May lived as if she were a side bar to the rest of us, but her sisters have never forgotten her and she is often on the phone with one or the other of them as they have become adults. For all of the hard choices that we had to make around her life, she still calls me every couple of weeks—to give me an update, she says. And in case you don't feel it between the lines of my writing I love her deeply but can't live with her successfully, even today.

LOVE GLUE

Chapter Eighteen

There is no smooth transition from May's place in our family to the other events that went on, so I will just move on.

The first Christmas in our new home was coming, and everyone wanted it to be special but children have a hard time expressing those kinds of thoughts. The year before Sy had scooped up a Christmas tree at a gas station and brought it home, but this year I needed to have a new tradition started; only I didn't know what I needed it to be. I was delighted when Sy said, "Let's bundle up the girls and go see if we can find a fresh tree to cut."

I passed on the message and started the girls moving to get on boots, jackets, find mittens and hats and be ready to leave when Sy had rounded up the necessary ropes and a saw for cutting our first real Christmas tree.

The girls reluctantly climbed up into our new shiny red van and sat down to await whatever. Fighting? You wouldn't believe the noise they could create. "Why do we have to do this?" was the question from one, and the next comment, "It's too cold out here." Then, "I can't go. I forgot my boots!" I don't think we waited around for the poor girl who didn't have boots; we just took off, headed for the country and a Christmas tree farm.

Pulling into the rutted frozen lot we saw smoke wisping from the chimney of a run-down, smoke-stained shack. Things quieted in the van. I drew in the woodsy smoke smell.

Sy said, "Let's see if they have a better saw and I'll check their prices while I'm at it."

Reluctant and grumpy teens tumbled from our vehicle. Inside the shack a potbellied stove radiated warmth while the smell of mulled cider drew the girls into the room. "Fresh made," the owner said, "You'll all have a cup when you get back?" The girls nodded--the first uncurling of their resistance to doing a 'family thing.'

Fetching the tree was involved, mostly because I kept vetoing the girls' choices while I looked for the most pregnant perfect tree. Over the ensuing years the girls have learned to pick out several trees knowing that Mother would have the final say. I must say Sy waited patiently while we scurried around through the other trees and the knee high snow to find that one and only tree. At last we agreed on a tree. Sy brushed away the snow at the base and then said, "You're sure now? This is the tree?" After the nods, he set about cutting and trimming the base. The tree bumped along behind Sy as he carried the butt-end while Cora, the oldest daughter, ran and jumped trying to hold up the tip.

I remember the cider being sweet-hot as we huddled in the shack, grateful for the break from the wind and snow. It was a welcome contrast to the bitter cold outside. Sy paid the man and the two of them wrestled the tree into the back of the van. When the girls were finished with their drinks they piled in around the beautiful snowy tree. We started off and everyone was silent. I was deep in the smell of Christmas and my memories of childhood holidays. From the back of the van, one girl's soft voice began the familiar words of an old Christmas carol. Two voices joined in—and finally everyone added their sound to the season.

This was the start of a family ritual that went on for years even to the youngest two girls' telephone call from their busy adult lives to see if we 'had gone for the tree yet'? I believe this was the family ritual that started our healing process, for two families, torn by divorce and beginning to heal in the warmth of two parents, who loved each other deeply and held their children in loving regard.

Christmas in its deepest sense is the re-honoring of the family. The Christian nativity scene is a symbolic embodiment of this idea with parents and friends standing in adoration of new life. Most religions carry this same theme. Can it be that the repetitive practice of a family ritual leads us back to a place of loving something beyond ourselves?

JessieMay Kessler

Christmas at Lakeview
Jordan Sanderson (Gramma Sands) Mother of Jessie
Joseph Baker (Grampa Joe) Sy's Ex-Father-in-Law

NUTS AND BOLTS

Chapter Nineteen

Some chapters in this book will be chronological story, some will be out of sequence because it reads better, and some will be explanation.

As Sy and I began to build our lives together, we had to change our vision from the dream of a perfect marriage to the reality of a blended family with difficult children, favorite children, and cooperative children—well, some of the time!

My children had lived under rules and regulations, most of which my ex-husband tried to undermine. Sy's children lived with rules that could be flexed or forgotten, so we had challenges.

I remember sitting at the dining room table one evening and Annie, our youngest, was moving the food around on her plate. As I watched, she did this for most of the meal, not eating much of anything except what she liked. Sy caught my eye but didn't say anything so, I played the role of bad cop and said, "Annie, my children have to eat everything on their plates but I see you don't like most of what you have been served. From now on everyone has to eat two bites of the food they are given."

She looked at her father and I held my breath.

"That's right," Sy said. "From now on everyone has to eat at least two bites of everything that is on their plate."

Annie responded, "Aw, Dad!" He nodded at her, which she knew meant the end of the subject.

That opened our eyes to the fact that there were many places in which the children had been trained by different standards. This led us to the Family Counsel Meeting, which was held twice a month on Sunday afternoon and was not optional. We gathered around the big maple dining room table while the chores for the two week period were listed. This list was composed by Sy and me during our coffee time in the evenings. The girls each got to choose one or two chores that they would complete each day. For this they were given an allowance each week. The lack of compliance was the loss of the allowance. Okay, this sounds perfect, but there was a lot of energy spent by parents checking to see that the chores were done. There had to be carry through.

The girls had access to the log book in which the chores were listed and they could write on the designated page any complaints they had against each other or the parents. These were brought up at the second half of the Sunday afternoon meetings. They could fight, quibble, or at least, be heard at these times. Sy would try to mediate, support, or redirect the girls to come to some resolution. I have to admit there were moments when he said, "Now, girls, this is the way it has to be!" He did lecture sometimes, but we were both guilty of that when we had the children's attention. I know, not the best approach but we weren't perfect as parents; we did try hard.

The next rule was that their allowance was not for spending all at once. A third of it had to go to their daily expenses, a third had to be saved, and a third was theirs to spend as they pleased. Some girls went through their money in the first day, some doled it out appropriately, and one never spent anything accept for daily expenses and then would not rescue another sister who was without money. Hey! They were miniature adults in training.

Another rule was that the beds had to be made before going off to school. Try implementing that, especially to girls facing the teen years. I soon learned that trying to straighten all those sheets and blankets was not going to happen. Too much work early in the morning!! So we switched to a bottom sheet and a warm quilt in a quilt cover, with whatever pillows they each needed. This system gave greater cooperation. We started the routine with no top sheet, but the quilt cover became so gross that I introduced the top sheet with some grumbling on their part.

I have the strong belief that children should have a healthy breakfast before starting off to school. So I got up at 5:45 a.m., a dreadful hour, and prepared a breakfast for all of them. I do admit that as time progressed, it was more what they liked to eat and less what was a 'healthy' breakfast. I also got breakfast for Sy and kissed him off to work around 7:00 a.m. My reward was to go back to bed to sleep for an hour more before facing my day. The system worked well because you have to remember that Sy and I were still new lovers in and around raising these children, so we often did not turn off the bedroom lights until late in the evening.

This brings me to another rule. We closed our bedroom door when we went to bed, something my girls had never experienced before and neither had Sy's girls, although mine complained more. We hung a sign on the bedroom door that read on one side "Lovers at Work" and on the other side "Come in, please." For many years the Lovers at Work side was there on Saturday mornings.

My adult daughter who was married last year for the second time, also creating a blended family, announced, "We don't have a sign because I hated that sign, but they have to knock until we tell them to come in." What did I say before about family rituals?

When I first began to date Sy, his youngest daughter, Annie, wanted to hold tightly to her father and announced this by trying to get between us physically--walk between, sit between and whatever worked at the time. The first instance when she tried this we were walking and I looked over her head and motioned with my eyes that Annie needed to move to his side and not be between us. He caught my message and moved her. Shortly, she gravitated back to between us. I looked at him again and he moved her. By the third try, she was beginning to get the message.

In church we refused to let any of the girls sit between us. I know it sounds cruel but it is a bit like the advice they give on air planes—the adult takes the oxygen first because if the adult can't function, the child is not going to survive. The outcome is that the girls knew from the start that Sy and I stood together on most issues, which I believe in the long run made for fewer discipline problems.

Speaking of church, the girls had to join us in church every Sunday and attend the youth group meetings in the evenings. You can imagine the complaining and groaning that went on! One Sunday evening Cora asked me, "Why do you make us go to Youth Group when we don't like church?"

My response was, "Honey, some day you are going to leave home and will be so home sick you won't know what to do with yourself. That is when you walk to the nearest church and you will suddenly have a built in family."

Just this year, as the mother of her own children, she told me that I was right in what I had said, and she attends church today. It didn't work as well with the others, but at least they don't feel awkward in a church service.

And, finally, the girls had to let us know where they were at all times; this was before cell phones. For the most part they complied. It made us trust them more when we got to the dating part which comes a little later in our story.

At the present time, I have been reading a chapter or two to whichever of the daughters is here visiting. Two days ago it was Annie. I told her I was going to write the chapter on the rules and asked her what she thought I should call it and she said, "The Green Prison 101?" From the grin on her face I think she was messing with me, at least I hope she was messing with me.

What she didn't know about was the time in the summer when Sy and I decided to take our coffee out to the front steps. We were sitting on the concrete, cups in hand, discussing and struggling with some problem of the girls that had raised its ugly head. The talk went back and forth and finally we felt we were at a workable solution. I turned to look out at the lovely gardens I had been working on during the morning. Suddenly, Sy slapped his leg. "Believe me, when they all turn eighteen there isn't going to be even one God-damned goldfish in this house!" We often held onto this thought as we moved forward, but as most of you know, there is always one more goldfish lurking in some corner with our adult off-spring.

I need to end this chapter with a back story to set up my story-time incident. When I was still at the old house in Grows Town alone with my daughters, there were times when I was having trouble getting my girls to do as I had asked of them. One day in utter frustration I said, "You're right! I am the Great Gray Witch!!" and walked away from the scene before me.

Fast forward to our lives as a blended family in Nerme--it had to have been about seven years into the marriage and Annie was a young teenager. I had scolded her for something and she stormed out of the kitchen. The next thing I knew she was stamping up the open stairway to the girls' second floor bed rooms. With each stomp I could hear her chanting, "The sisters are right! She is the Great Gray Witch!"

LEARNING TO LISTEN

Chapter Twenty

We had not been residents of the big 'ugly green house' for too many months when the women in the community planned a dessert hour to meet the new women in that area known as Green Trees. I'm not great on social get-togethers, but I felt it was important for me to attend this one since I really didn't know many people in Nerme Town. The women were cordial and the desserts were sinful. One woman searched me out and started a conversation.

"I know you moved into the big house on the corner. Do you have children?"

I responded, "Yes I have five daughters all in or approaching the teen years."

"I feel for you. What are their names," she asked?

"Well, the oldest is Cora. She's in high school."

"She is pretty and has long blond hair? She waits out on the corner for the bus?"

"Yes, that would be Cora," I responded.

"I know her. I'd recognize her as your daughter anywhere. She looks just like you!"

I thanked her. We talked a bit more and then she was off to welcome someone else.

When I got home I shared my afternoon with Cora and we had a great laugh together.

Since I was a stay-at-home Mom at that time, when the girls got home from school they would come to find me and I quickly learned that it was snack and tea time. I needed to sit and listen while they talked. At first they would descend on me in about the same time frame and talk all at once. I had to ask them to take turns talking, but the interesting thing is they gradually set their own time to come and visit after school.

Cora got home from high school before the others so she was first. Elizabeth, still in junior high, would come next for a short while. Then the two younger girls were home from grade school and Felicia would appear first. By the time it was Annie's turn, I was often getting supper, so she would fanny-up on the counter at the outer corner of my U shaped kitchen and talk as I was preparing supper. Would you believe, Annie often calls me, to this day, at the time that was her private time with Mother—while I'm getting supper?

It was before Easter of this first year together and because I had been brought up with new clothes and new shoes for Easter, I elected to take all four of the girls out to get new shoes at the same time. Here we are in the shoe store. There are at least twenty shoe boxes and twice as many shoes strewn out around our feet. Little voices are chirping, "Moon, are these long enough. Would you check the toes?" "Mummy, can I have this color? I love this color!" Meanwhile one girl, eyes glued to her new shoes, has wandered off to the far end of the store. The clerk had to round her up. Someone else was saying, "Can we get more than one pair of shoes?"

Before we were done, I had a headache par excellent! Gradually the clerk and I worked with each girl until they seemed satisfied, but when I was reviewing our trip at coffee time with Sy, he said with his wonderful engineer's wisdom, "So I'm assuming you will never take them out again, all at once?"

I responded, "You'd better believe it. I learned a big lesson today."

Out of this incident a new rule was born. You never talk to Mom all at once if you want to be heard. You take turns, and if you are with other people, you listen and speak when they are done. Only one person talks at a time. Did Annie call it the Green Prison? It was a matter of survival and a mother's sanity that seemed to only be able to hear one child at any given moment.

I need to tell you that the girls did not call me Mom or Mother or Jessie. I never told them who I was other than telling them in the beginning that I was not Mrs. Lesser. In the beginning Cora asked if she could call me Moon. That was fine with me so long as she would talk to me and she did. My biological daughters called me Mom or Mummy. May called me Ma, which I hated, because that name drew me back to my childhood and the people that my mother always told me were 'from the other part of town.' It sounded like she was a child of the 'streets' to me. And, of course, once she knew I didn't like it she made a point to refer to me that way. To her credit, with the years and some maturity, she now calls me Mom. Annie just left that space blank for a while, but she was the first of the two step-daughters to convert to calling me Mom. I add this tender point because I have sat with other blended families in the counseling room and a big issue is sometimes made that the children will not call the maternal figure in the home Mom. They can't because their loyalties are mixed. As relationship is cultivated and grows, they come up with their own comfortable term for the Mother.

I will weave more of the girls' lives in as we proceed with the story and it may seem as if Sy has moved to the background. He was never in the back ground, he was beside me; he was the foundation of this pillar of feminine development and the security that made it possible for we women to reach for our potential.

Speaking of a pillar of feminine energy, we went into family counseling early on in the marriage. The therapist was a young male and we were to assemble for a group meeting. Sy arrived first and like many mothers my car-full was late. The therapist asked Sy if it was a problem being the only male in an all-female household. Sy hesitated for a moment and then responded, "Well, Hobo the dog is male." We didn't stay long with that therapist.

I'm sure Sy's flip response came before that evening when we were at supper around the dining room table. Cora usually sat to one side of her father who was at the head of the table and Felicia sat next to Cora with Elizabeth on the other side of Sy and Annie next to me. We are conversing, and eating, and suddenly Cora launches into a conversation about her menstrual cycle. I look at Sy, he looks back at me from his end of the table in horror and I have to make a swift decision—do I shut down the freedom to talk about a subject that affects everyone but Sy, teaching all of the girls a conservative, uptight view on body and sexuality? I chose to be open and asked her a question which she happily answered and went on. I'm watching Sy at his end of the table somehow slip lower and lower in his chair. We chuckled together afterwards but I do not think he felt it was one of the more comfortable table conversations.

I want to end this chapter with what I believe is the core response of each adult daughter if they were asked what is your life mantra? Now I expect they might disagree but it will give you a mini outline of their personalities as we move forward.

Cora—"Do you love me?"

May—"I want to come home, but I won't stop the drinking. I'm not ready."

Elizabeth—"I don't need anything."

Felicia—"Do you have a moment to talk?"

Annie—"What can I do to help?"

THE BOTTOM LINE

Chapter Twenty-One

The church service that we usually attended as a family was fairly early in the day and getting four or five girls to eat breakfast, wash faces, apply makeup, and put clothes on, just didn't happen. So we tended to skip breakfast and simply go to church. After the service Sy would bring us home and then he would make a trip into town to get his Sunday paper, a box of donuts and scrumptious other pastries from the bakery.

Thinking back, I realize that was a horrible Sunday brunch to serve young people, but it tasted so good and the girls devoured every piece. I am supposing that that much sugar at one time could change people's moods quickly. Whatever, we were all sitting around the table talking and I must have said something, which I don't remember now.

Elizabeth erupted with "You fucking bitch!"

I was stunned and confused. Elizabeth tended to be quiet in the family.

Sy looked at her in consternation and said, "What did you say?"

Elizabeth responded, "You heard me. She's a fucking bitch!"

"You will apologize to your mother right now." Sy commanded.

"No! I won't. She's a bitch!"

He retorted, "Apologize!"

Elizabeth looked at him as if sizing up where he really was on the matter.

Through clenched teeth Sy said, "Go to your room!"

Again, Elizabeth hesitated but as she heard his chair push out from the table, she was up and scrambling for the stairs. Sy was right behind her, I think taking two steps to her running three. From downstairs you could hear her bedroom door slam and the scrape of a chair being pulled across the floor. My heart sank in my chest. This was a step-father who had never before been challenged with such a test of his firmness and temper control in front of his whole new family. I wanted to go to where I could protect my daughter, if need be, but I knew that this had to play out for the stability of our newly blended family. Then we, who were sitting at the table, heard the unmistakable three well placed swats. In a few minutes Sy returned to the table, looked at me, and sat down in his place. We all heaved a sigh and finished eating our donuts. The pleasure had vanished.

Elizabeth didn't come down to join us for supper, unheard of in our household. She did appear for breakfast with her sisters, her face puffy and eyes red from crying for much of the time. No one spoke to her and she didn't speak to any of us. It was on the second morning that she quietly said to me at the breakfast table, "I'm sorry, Mum."

And I responded, "Apology accepted."

I know, I know, spanking is no longer an acceptable punishment in many present day households. And I'm not advocating spanking a child when some other measure would change the behavior, but part of what Elizabeth was doing was asking 'where are the boundaries in this new family? Who is in charge? Who is going to set limits and protect me from myself? What is the bottom line?' At that moment in our family's development, a spanking by her step-father was what she needed. I believe over the years Elizabeth has grown to love and respect Sy deeply and is still mourning, in her own way, his sudden death.

My relationship with Elizabeth has always been a yo-yo relationship. When she was little she was at my side most of the time. She was my 'apron string' child. Then, when she was nine, I asked her father for a divorce.

Harvard refused to tell the children as he went about buying a new house and spending many hours on the far side of the block preparing that new space for his move.

I finally said to him, "Harvard, this can't go on. The girls know something is wrong and we have to tell them now, today."

May was visiting with my mother, so only Elizabeth and Felicia were available. We sat them down in the living room on the couch, Harvard taking his place between them. He put his arm around Elizabeth's shoulders and said, "Your mother doesn't love me anymore. She wants me to get out." Elizabeth turned to look at him in disbelief and to soak in what he was saying. I believe in that instant she emotionally became 'his wife.' I was so dumbfounded at the martyrdom in his presentation that I said nothing to counteract the results.

It had to have been about a month after Harvard had moved and it was raining hard outside, actually it had been raining for several days. Elizabeth came to me and said, "Mummy, why does it have to rain all the time?" Instinctively I knew she was asking about more than just rain. I sat down in front of our then large picture window and pulled her onto my lap so we could both watch the rain as it hit the glass and slid down to the gardens below. "It has to rain so that God can give the plants the water they need to drink. If we didn't have rain we wouldn't have the tulips that come in the spring." Her only response was, "Oh, okay," as we continued to watch, together.

Elizabeth was the first daughter to go off to college and we had visited schools the previous spring. She settled on a small school in Bunker City, and while we were waiting for her entrance interview, we walked up and down Brad's Street looking in the windows at the various shops. We came to a basement level boutique and she wanted to go in. The clerk asked if she could help us and I told her we were waiting for my daughter's interview at French Junior College.

The woman asked Elizabeth, "Do you know what you want to do when you finish with your college degree?"

Elizabeth took a quick visual tour of the shop and said, "I want to have this; a small shop of my own." I was amazed because she had never before put into words what she planned to do with her adult life.

She was accepted and Sy and I drove all her college baggage to her dormitory during that ensuing fall. She rode with her high school sweetheart, Jon. I remember that she was placed in a double room on the fifth floor. It was a garret of a room, and when I saw it, my heart sank. The built-in isolation! It was her first time away from home and me--other than summer vacations with her father and his wife. We got her settled in as best we could in such a tiny space and the moment had come to say good-bye. I started to hug her and she drew me into a neighboring vacant room and as I took her into my arms my stoic daughter, who stood taller than I, nearly collapsed. She clung to me and I clung to her. --One of the more torturous moments in my life next to Sy's death. Then she turned away and I knew I had to gather myself up and find where Sy was waiting to take the five flights down to our parked car.

There are high school graduations, boyfriends, and weddings farther on in our story but I want to end this chapter on Elizabeth with something that illustrates the 'yo-yoness' of our relationship.

I hadn't had contact with Elizabeth for months. She was married or coming out of her divorce, I'm not sure of the exact time in this story, but she showed up for our big Christmas morning unwrapping-of-the-gifts. She put her bag of goodies for people under the tree and Sy did his usually job of handing out presents, one at a time, so that we would have a chance to savor what we had received. At one point he handed me a package that felt like a picture and said, "The tag says this is from Elizabeth."

I unwrapped the gift and it was both a picture and a poem, actually a plaque, which I must share with you.

Family

No matter how great the distance, we return;
Bearing the bruises of the paths we've chosen.
....
We take comfort in knowing
We are surrounded by...all we need . . . each other.
By Tom Tarrant

This has been abridged due to the copyright laws.

A Bird and the Dragon: Their Love Story

Elizabeth Hugging her Step-sister Cora at One of the Weddings

WHO'S RUNNING THE HOUSE?

Chapter Twenty Two

Sy and I had been married for a year and this was January of 1979. Life was so peaceful in this new situation that I became restless. Both the children and I had become so used to emotional disruption that sometimes I discovered I was missing that disjointed energy. Sounds crazy! But I did notice that if things ran smoothly for too long, the girls would create some kind of upset. Talk about conditioning!

Cora and I were getting along but I could feel the tension building. In her original home she had been pretty much in charge of her father's household while keeping an eye on her little sister, Annie. I sensed that if I didn't change things up, we would grow to be at odds. So I said to Sy one evening at coffee, "I'd like to go back to school and get my master's degree in counseling. I've always been the listener and I think I could do this."

"I think it's a great idea," he responded. "Do you have any sense of where you want to go?"

"No, I don't even know what I need for a background and who would accept me."

"Looks like you have some research to do, but I do believe you can do it. Go for it."

I forget now how I did the research because we had no computer yet, but I found that Saint Anthony's College in Bushnell City had a degree in Pastoral Counseling. Having been a minister's wife for thirteen years, I thought I might have the necessary credentials. I took the test to see if I qualified to even study at the master's level and was amazed that I aced the exam fifteen years after I'd left undergraduate school.

A Bird and the Dragon: Their Love Story

I went for my interviews, gathered my previous school records, and was accepted. I took one course that semester at Sy's suggestion because we didn't know how the girls would accept this change and how I would manage driving back and forth to Bushnell City one day a week while maintaining a busy household.

The interesting thing about academic logic is after the first class, we were told we had to go out and find clients to counsel. It sounds easy enough, but in most states, if you don't have a degree or a license, no one will hire you. I can often be brought to a halt by this kind of problem, but with Sy encouraging me, I went to the YWCA and asked if they would like me to run a course for people going through a divorce. They said 'yes' and then I asked if I could have any of the students that came out of that group as potential clients. They agreed and we were off and moving forward.

Not only was I doing classes, I was also structuring and running an information workshop. We brought in experts to speak on various issues facing people in divorce and the series was a success. I also got a few clients.

Would you believe while this was happening, Cora decided that she really didn't want to run my household or be accountable for her new sisters? Problem solved.

As the second semester rolled around it became clear that I would have to be away from home two late afternoons and evenings a week for two years. Sy and I came up with the plan that each girl would cook the dinner one night a week. They would submit a menu plan and their grocery list one week ahead so that I could do the food shopping. This gave me time to attend classes and to study on the days when I wasn't in class. Sy supervised the girls when I was away and those that didn't cook took turns filling the dishwasher. He or I did pots and pans when we could get to the sink. It worked well and it taught the girls how to cook without Mother hovering over their shoulders making corrections and suggestions. They took advice from their father/step-father far better than they would have from me. The down side was that by the end of my tour in college, Sy announced that he didn't care if he ever saw another hot dog, lima bean or any spaghetti O's.

Somewhere at the end of that second semester, one of the school officials came to me and told me that they were sorry that I did not qualify to be a pastoral counselor because I had to have been a minister with ministerial training before I could gain that degree. I was devastated because I'd already invested time and money. They told me they would do some more research and see if I would qualify for a straight counseling degree and the upshot was that I did. --So much for thirteen years as the minister's wife!

The next-to-last semester consisted of learning how to work with clients and to present, before the class, a client and the work that we had been doing together. There is a phenomenon in counseling called transference and counter transference. The first situation is when the client perceives you as the offending parent and projects all of that negative material onto you. The second situation is when you, the therapist, sees the client as someone in your life and then project your material onto the client.

When I got to that particular class on the first day I was delighted to find my professor was Rev. Felix Davis. He was a contemporary of Rev. David Eaton, the man who had been the therapist for Sy and me. Felix was also a Jungian in counseling orientation. I felt at home in his class. He began to recognize as he called on students and I would answer that I understood his thinking.

The day came for me to make my presentation of my client. I chose a man from the workshop I had conducted. As I began to set out what was happening in sessions and what he was and wasn't accomplishing, I began to cry. I felt utterly stupid and that I was destroying my chance to be a practicing therapist.

Felix saw my discomfort and said, "Go on. You are presenting one of the best examples I have ever seen of the counter transference at work. When did your father die?" With this compassionate approach on his part, I was able to finish my presentation, although I still felt I might have ruined my career as a therapist.

It was the last semester and I was having trouble with one of my clients. I was not able to move them forward in their therapeutic journey and so made an appointment to see the professor who was the acting head of the counseling program. When the day came, I was ushered into Dr. Decamps' office and left to wait. His secretary sat at her desk at the back of his long narrow office. I waited and waited. Finally Dr. Decamp arrived and took a chair, swung it around so he was straddling the chair and facing me. He asked, "Now what can I do for you?"

I started describing the problem I was having and he stopped me in mid-sentence, "How are you feeling?"

I was surprised but said, "I'm feeling fine." I'm having this problem with my client and I don't understand why we are stuck."

"How are you feeling?" Dr. Decamp asked again.

"I'm fine, a little frustrated with this client. That's why I came to you."

"So how are you feeling?"

"I told you I'm feeling fine!" I responded.

"No, I'm asking how are you feeling, right now?"

"I'm angry and frustrated because you are not solving my problem!"

"How are you feeling?" Dr. Decamp asked once more.

By now the tears were streaming down my face. I felt like a fool and I didn't understand why he was harassing me. I grabbed my file folder and bolted from the room. The secretary didn't bat an eye as I rushed by her. Once out in the hall I realized that my next class was in the room across the hall with Dr. Decamp. Talk about humiliation. I sat close to the door in case I had to jump and run again.

The professor went through the usual introductory procedures for the class and then he said, "It has come to my attention that some of you are not in touch with your own feelings and if you can't recognize your own feelings, how can you align yourself with and recognize the feelings of your client?"

It was as if a light was turned on. I grew up in a household where no one talked about or even recognized that they had feelings. My family functioned from the top of the head down to the neck and no farther. Everything was always shoveled under the rug, so to speak. In a sense we were taught to 'make nice.'

The dreaded practicum came toward the end of my course work with Dr. Decamp. We had to find some place where we could go as students and practice being a therapist. Where was I going to find a situation like that when I lived so far away from Bushnell City? I came home with my depressing problem. Sy listened, and in one brilliant move, said, "Why don't you ask Felix if you can come to work for him?"

"After the way I fell apart in his class, I don't think he will want me in his counseling center."

"Well, you'll never know if you don't ask. Nothing ventured, nothing gained. I dare you to ask him."

Never give me a dare; it is the prod that will move me forward. At the next class I arrived early and walked up to Felix as he stood ready to start the class. "I'm supposed to find a practicum and I wondered if I could come and work for you?" I asked with baited breath. I focused on his mass of white hair while waiting for the rejection.

"I've been thinking something along the same lines," he said. "But you understand we are a counseling center, so the other members will have to vote on your becoming a part of our group."

My legs went weak and I wasn't sure I could get back to my seat. "Oh, thank you," I mumbled, not convinced that I could get the words out correctly.

At class two weeks later, Felix called me aside. He had talked to the other counselors at the center and they agreed they were ready to take on some new blood. I not only had my practicum settled, I had my first official job.

It was about three days before I was to graduate and Dr. Decamp called me into his office. "I've been looking over your course work and I'm not sure I can graduate you with all of this Jungian stuff that you have been using on your clients. We don't teach Carl Jung here at Saint Anthony's."

I was stunned. I'm sure it was my guides, but the next thing I said was, "Dr. Davis has offered me a job at the Medfield Pastoral Counseling Center in Medfield, Connecticut. Is that enough for me to graduate?"

"Oh, well. I wasn't aware of that fact. Yes, I suppose if you already have a job with one of our professors I have to graduate you."

So much for Dr. Decamp!!

Sy and my mother attended my graduation. When the ceremony was over, my mother leaned into me and said, "Now, will you be satisfied?" She was referring to my restless spirit, always reaching for the next adventure, but she could have said, "Boy, you have done a great job to be in a second marriage, raise a family, and still get your master's degree." You can see how I didn't learn how to voice feelings as a child. She wasn't able to recognize or tell me that she was jealous of my success.

ROCKS IN THE BOAT

Chapter Twenty-Three

My chapter title does not mean that our boat had rocks or that the children were rocks in our marriage; it means that we needed to get the boat balanced.

When a person trains to be a therapist, it only makes sense that they are in counseling themselves. How else can you know what it feels like for the client? Most of us have baggage we need to deal with rather than possibly unloading it onto a client. So, as I went back into counseling, it became even more obvious that our children also needed help.

Both families had moved out of chaotic, dysfunctional homes. So over the three years that I was training I was also running girls to various therapists. They didn't all go in the same time frame but it did mean that my late afternoons, not spent at school, were spent on the road getting each girl to what we felt were superior therapists. Elizabeth seemed to work better with male therapists and they were more expensive than the female therapists. Time hasn't changed things all that much!!

Harvard was supposed to cover my girl's medical expenses, but over time we discovered that he never seemed to have the necessary paper work or he forgot to send it in or some other excuse. Sy just put all the girls on his medical plan. But even with this insurance help, the girl's work was costly.

I regret that I didn't push more afterschool programs, getting the girls involved in extracurricular activities, but our lives seemed to be full without them. Home work was important and they were expected to sit down after their visit time with me and study around the dining room table until the work was done. I'm sure when I was off at school the dining room table was vacant. But even at that, three of the girls went on to get associates degrees and Cora, who chose to leave the home early, tried to go back later and get her degree.

So far I think I've made our home sound like a smooth running machine, but it wasn't. There were disagreements among the girls, and Sy and I also had our differences. Ours seemed to circle around the two youngest girls—the his 'n her twins. If you should ask our grown daughters why, they would answer, 'Because Annie was Dad's favorite kid and Felicia was your favorite kid.' And I would have to agree that we did function that way. We would each stand and defend our own whether it was sensible to do that or not.

I can remember one super fight after we had moved the first time. Sy and I were standing in the new kitchen—I by the sink and he at the end of the peninsula. As he is roaring, I'm thinking to myself, 'this is like it was with Harvard. I don't think Sy loves me anymore.' At that moment Sy pounded the counter with his clenched fist and said, "And you know what? A hundred years from now we won't remember what this fight was about!" I looked at him and he looked up at me and we both broke into peals of laughter. He was right. I don't remember what started the fight or even what it was about.

If my memory serves me, we didn't fight as much after that. We did more discussion and working to see the other person's view. We each gave in more or maybe Sy decided that a happy wife meant a happy life. Whatever, our relationship was smoother until we had the store. That is later in the story.

One of the rules that I didn't mention in the Nuts and Bolts section was that the girls were not allowed to fight with each other during the dinner meal; that was a matter for the Family Counsel. The dinner table had been a war zone in both previous families and I did not wish to set up disrupted digestive tracts, so fights were for after we left the table.

Speaking of the dinner table, in my childhood home my mother and my sister carried the conversation. When I did enter into the conversation I was often off track because I was so much younger than everyone else and I was either ignored or my older siblings would laugh. I learned not to talk at the table.

When I married Harvard, I soon experienced that he was anxious in public situations and so monopolized the conversation. When we got to the blended family, I learned, in retrospect, that I had at least two girls with Bipolar disorder and anxiety is heightened for them if the environment is silent, so Cora controlled the conversations.

At one point, Elizabeth came to me and said, "Can't we get her to shut up?" I responded, "I'm the step-mother. But what you can do is search around during your day for a topic that might interest people. Then at diner ask your step-father something about your topic. I think he will talk with you and block her in the process." Elizabeth did this for a while and it worked, but after time, it became too much of a job.

As we move forward in the story I have to mention that I have a restless spirit—witness my mother's comment at my graduation--and after about five to ten years in one home, I need to find something that seems to fit better. Maybe I'm a creature that needs to shed what I know and grow a new skin every so many years. Looking back, I realize that I had a marvelous husband who would say, "You know I hate to move;" then he would set his shoulder to the process and walk with me through all the problems until we were in a new environment.

THE LITTLE BIRD

Chapter Twenty-Four

I was deep in the midst of school and Sy pointed out to me that we didn't see much of his mother except on the holidays and it would be nice if we invited her to dinner some evening.

I found a night when I was not at school so that I could do the cooking. I had made dinner preparations and the sink was full of pots and pans but it was time to take one of the girls to a counseling appointment. I was out of butter. I called Sy and asked him to pick up three items including the butter and his mother on his way home from work. I'd be home in time to finish up the meal and be a pleasant hostess. What do they say about the best laid plans of mice and men?

The therapist kept whichever child it was overtime, there was heavy traffic coming home, and I arrived to find that Gramma Celia was already there and my handsome husband was laid out under the kitchen sink up to his "proverbial" elbows in water and not in the best of moods.

Someone had tried to help me by running the food disposal in the sink. They had turned on the water as you are supposed to do and turned on the switch to the disposal. It jammed! And to make matters worse, Celia had the need to come and check the mess in my sink and how her son was progressing. Did I say she was practical?

We solved the problem by washing what was needed in a bathroom sink and Sy tackled the food grinder after Gramma Celia had returned home. The cooked food must have been good because my mother-in-law never made mention of our disastrous attempt at entertaining her.

A Bird and the Dragon: Their Love Story

That year we had Christmas together as usual, but Gramma Celia did not seem as alert as in times past, although she seemed to enjoy being with us and she watched the children's antics with apparent pleasure. My mother was there also and they chatted off and on. I remember that we held Christmas in the family room that year so it was a more relaxed affair—not that we ever were very formal except at Thanksgiving.

It was in the spring of 1981 when Sy became aware that his mother was not feeling well. He took her in to the doctor for an examination, which resulted in a trip to the hospital. There they did surgery and some rerouting of intestines which resulted in her going back into surgery a few months later to be reconnected properly. At that time they found there was cancer and enough that she was not a candidate for extensive treatment. By now she was not going to be able to care for herself so Sy found a nursing home in Comfortville and placed her in their keeping. She was not there for very long.

I was free this particular afternoon and went to visit her. She was sleeping, so I stood quietly to see if she would wake. I spoke to her, but she didn't respond. I stood and waited. She finally opened her eyes, recognized who I was, and asked, "Did you see them?"

"Gramma Celia, did I see who?" I asked.

"My brothers and sisters! Did you see them?"

"No, Celia, I didn't see them but I know you did and they are waiting for you to return."

She murmured something and then asked for a drink of water. I tried to give her the paper cup of water but she was too weak to hold it. I then tried to hold it for her and spilled it down on her neck and shoulder. I felt so terrible and apologized profusely.

"It's not a problem," she said as she reached up with her hand to comfort me. It is an embarrassing and tender memory for me.

I called for the attendants to come and dry her off and then I said my good-byes. I returned home and got the children organized to do their supper cooking while I went down to finish a load of laundry in the basement.

I heard Sy returning from work upstairs; then the telephone rang. He walked to the telephone in the hall right above my head. In about five minutes I heard his footsteps coming down the cellar stairs. One look at his face and I knew what had been said on the telephone. He walked into my arms and stood sobbing. In a few minutes he pulled himself together and went back upstairs. That was the extent of his public grieving.

He made the call to the Rabbi and the man came to visit us the next afternoon. The Rabbi talked to us about the service and explained the various parts because he understood that Sy was no longer a practicing Jew. When he was finished preparing us for the next day, he asked if we wanted to know what Celia's name meant in Hebrew and of course we answered 'yes.'

He said, "It means Little Bird."

I looked at Sy and he looked at me. If you remember, my mother had refused to let go of calling me by my nick-name which was Birdie. Not only was I called Birdie but my grandmother Mary Emma saw me running across the lawn with arms outstretched as a toddler and said, "Oh, here comes my little bird."

Sy did not mourn at the service or outwardly at any other time. We went for a few visits to where she was buried and he showed me how, if you are Jewish, you carry a stone and place it on the grave. But over time the cemetery gates were never open so you had to scale the stone wall and we went less and less. One day I mentioned the lack of visiting and he said, "You know she is around us, here. She couldn't bear not to keep an eye on all of this."

TIME ALONE

Chapter Twenty-Five

I'm not sure when Sy and I married that we were fully prepared for how much work it would be to raise five girls in a blended family. We soon learned that like the parent on the airplane, we needed to find a source of oxygen to replenish ourselves and build stamina for the next leg of the journey. That began to be a week away during the February school vacation—a celebration of our wedding anniversary. My mother (bless her endurance) came and stayed with the girls on most occasions.

Before I met Sy, I had been visiting with my three girls at my sister's farm in Central Vermont. This particular day she suggested that when I drove home I should go through Woodstock, Vermont, to get a flavor for the town. I did as she instructed and felt at home. The old homes and small shops along the main street—the quintessential wealthy New England village—and I wanted to stay, but I could smell the fact that my wish would require more money than a single mother with children could muster.

When Sy began making noises that he felt we needed a break and where did I think I wanted to go, Woodstock came to mind. He did the research and we spent a week at the Woodstock Inn right in the center of town. --Beautiful accommodations and food to write home about. We arrived late on a Sunday afternoon, in time for tea and cookies or a bite to eat in the dining room. We chose the dining room which was sectioned into a main area and a breakfast room. We sat in the breakfast room and the waitress brought the day's special dessert—a slice of pumpkin roll cake filled with a scrumptious cream type filling and a daub of whipped cream on the top. The hint of nutmeg was just enough to send it over the top and I can still taste it as I write.

We poked in the shops and looked at the jewelry—a major downfall for me. We toured the working dairy farm and spoke to the new kittens. Sy found the general store and it contained anything you could not find anywhere else in New England. The weekend evenings ended with dinner at one of the fine restaurants in the area, particularly The Prince and the Pauper. A brisk walk home through lightly falling snow and then bursting into the Inn to see and feel the roar of their almost walk-in fireplace, warmed the whole stone lobby area, a fitting finish to the day. If that did not feed the souls of two lovers, I'm not sure what it would have taken. The best part of our vacations was that we didn't have to do anything—we could have just sat in the room and talked. I never went on a trip with Sy when I didn't have a great time. As I said, he liked to shop and, being more adventuresome than I, he was willing to explore wherever we went.

We went back to Woodstock many times, but it was in the spring of 1982 when Sy decided he wanted some other type of vacation and so we moved our trip to the April vacation and went to Williamsburg, Virginia. Sy should have been a history or English teacher because he loved all kinds of history, most particularly our American History. We toured the various shops, saw some of the trades' men at work, but the place that held his interest the longest was a display of artifacts found under and around one of the buildings when they were refurbishing it to be a place for the public.

Each article was mounted with an explanation of what the article was, what it was used for, and where it had been found. I'm not into history—I'm on the street corner waiting for the next future invention. But even I found Williamsburg and that display very interesting. We ended our day with an authentic dinner at one of the taverns. The ambiance was delightful but the food was bland. It was possible to sit in the flickering candle light and imagine what it was like in times past for soldiers or dignitaries to be passing through the town.

I love my children dearly but it was hard to come to the end of a vacation and head home to all the details that made life good for our girls.

MILE STONES

Chapter Twenty-Six

Cora graduated from Nerme high school in June of 1982. We weren't able to convince her that she needed to go on to more education. She was set on getting a job and becoming independent. She did get a job in Nerme Village. Fearful that she would become a permanent fixture in our home, we decided that each girl would get a year at home free after their last school graduation and then they were expected to find a place of their own. Because she had not chosen to go on in school, that cut off-point was fast approaching and she began picking fights with her father. It didn't matter who walked into the room first, someone said something and they were into it.

During one session with my therapist I was asking why suddenly all the fighting and both of them were instigating this foolishness. Jane Summers, my then therapist, paused for a moment and said, "Each child in the family chooses one parent or the other to drive them out of the home. Didn't you know that?" Once she spoke the words, I could see how it had played out in the generations before.

I'm not sure what sparked this particular incident but I believe we told Cora that since she was growing towards time to leave us, she needed to start doing her own laundry and we would begin to ask for weekly rent in a certain low figure which we would return when she left. She became so mad at us that she stormed out of the house, walked into town, rented a room in a rooming house for twice what we were asking, and came back to claim her things. It didn't take long for her to return to visit with me and to tell me how poor the situation was, but that she was proud that she could be independent. And I agreed with her, as I hurt for and admired her stubborn pride.

That same year Felicia turned fourteen in the spring and Annie turned fourteen in June. Birthdays were a family time with cake, ice cream, candles and gifts. Felicia had hers in the dining room around the maple table. She invited a girlfriend from school and Grampa Joe also came.

Annie had her birthday celebration outside on the brick patio that Sy had built when we put in the pool. She invited some friends and the major part of the time was in the pool swimming, if you could call it that.

Elizabeth turned sixteen in July that same year and had never been out there socially, so I made much of a sixteenth birthday and hung a huge pair of stuffed pink lips in the center of the outside umbrella. I think she was embarrassed but enjoyed the attention and of course everyone that came swam in the pool and ate cake and ice cream.

I spoke before about being a restless spirit and this was the start of the next move. The television was talking about the oncoming shortage in gas and I began to think that perhaps it would be better if we lived closer to town where we could walk to anything we really needed. Sy was away on a testing run and I was driving into town to do my groceries. I looked down the side street that ran beside our church and saw there was a For Sale sign on a scruffy looking house lot. I drove down and was amazed at the price but still it seemed high to me. When Sy called that evening I told him about the land and the price and that I thought it was high.

To my amazement he said, "So call up the listing agent and offer what you think it is worth."

"But you don't like to move," I countered.

"You're right, but I know you have been thinking about this for a while and it will be good to see if you can get what you want."

With great fear I made the call, got the agent, laid out my thoughts and the agent told me it was an estate sale. There were four parties involved and it might take some time, especially where I wasn't interested in paying list price.

The upshot was that Sy was home and there were calls back and forth and the people sold the land for what I was offering. He had a lot of kind words for me. That was before we went and walked the land. The whole front of the lot was ledge—more than anyone would want to blast—but we were pleasantly surprised to see how far back and to the side the land ran. We had gotten a deal if we could find a house plan to fit the lot and a builder.

Talking about this new adventure, someone in the church said they had used a contractor named Ben and were very pleased with his work. They invited us to their house after church for a tour and some talk about specifics. We appreciated the quality of workmanship and their only complaint was that he was slow to come and touch up places that had been finished in haste. –Small problem for us at that point.

We put a call in to Ben and he said he was interested. He wanted a floor plan and a chance to walk the land. I had been hoarding a house plan that I had found in the newspaper. It was a Cape Cod house with some modern twists like two sliding doors across the front of the house and a cathedral ceiling in the living room which ran into a loft area for the girls' bedrooms. He sat with us and our plan and then said he would have to draw up his own version with the changes we wanted, and while he was doing that, he wanted us to clear the land. The large trees he would cut if needed, but he didn't like to drop too many trees. We agreed.

That fall we set to work clearing the land and I believe much of my present day back problems are from holding a bush whacker for hours at a time while I cleared the smaller brush and Sy worked at cutting or chopping the larger inhabitants of that gorgeous spot.

Building began in earnest the following year.

BUILDING A HOUSE

Chapter Twenty-Seven

The construction of our new house began in earnest in the spring of 1984. Ben found that the only way to logically situate the house on the lot was to blast a small portion of the front rocky cliff area. This would allow for the entranceway of the house through the breezeway. That blasting was done while the earth was still cold.

During the winter Ben had been tinkering with our floor plans and had come up with some really neat features. Since the house faced southeast, in the living room behind those sliding glass doors the floor would be laid in a terra cotta tile to allow for passive solar heating. Then, in the breeze way, he designed it to be extra wide to accommodate a small indoor pool with sky lights above to help with the possible ventilation problem. In the kitchen I wanted a fire place but the kitchen was on the small side so the fireplace was designed to sit at hip height and backed onto the breeze way. There was both a prep area and a shaker trestle table in that kitchen with a clerestory glass panel as the ceiling at the ceiling/wall junction above both areas. Informal dinners in the warmer months were often lighted by the setting sun.

If you should come into the home through the sliders you would see a wide brick pillar raising the whole height of the house. There was an open balcony that ran along the second floor level at the back of the house to make a corridor for the girls' bedrooms. They loved the fact that the corridor ran behind that brick pillar where they could hide and watch what was going on down below in the open dining/living room area. By this time boy friends had entered the picture. What a great place from which to spy!

One of the other reasons for moving to a new location was to have a dedicated office for my counseling practice. So at the back of the house there was a small porch that connected the kitchen to the garage. For me it was a short walk to the front part of the garage and up an enclosed stairway to my office complex above the garage.

For anxious owners, a house never emerges fast enough from the ground. The framing was up and Ben's builders had started on the roof rafters of the house when we had three days of rain onto the subfloor of what was going to be our dining room floor. When it looked as if the storm would be over Sy and I drove to the house with buckets and scooped out the ankle deep water. I had much to say about how this was going to warp and destroy the base of the dining room floor. Sy was quiet. By now he recognized it was best to let me have my rant. And as we finally finished scooping and tossing water out the slider doors, Sy looked up and said, "See it's going to work out all right. Look at that rainbow!"

Somewhere in our family picture album there is a picture of Sy and I sitting on the floor in the eventual living room having a picnic. I was feeling down about the progress of the house and Sy said, "We don't have any kids here right now. Let's pack a lunch and go eat it in our new house." And that's why the picture. He always knew what would lift my spirits or that I needed my spirits lifted.

We did the packing up of the 'ugly green house' and called in a real estate agent to start the process of selling the big house. She made some minor suggestions about staging which we accomplished and then put the house up for sale. Within a month's time the place had sold. Our new house was far from finished. We put the buyers off for one month but that was all they would give us.

On to plan B! We put most of our belongings into storage and got out the camping equipment. Sy, in the past, had built me a camping kitchen cabinet and that was placed at the end of our picnic table in the back yard of our new home. We had an eating canopy that he set up and my temporary kitchen evolved under that semi tent. He set up the larger tent for the three remaining girls while we occupied the smaller tent. The rub was that the girls were still going to school as the academic year had not quite ended. Sy rigged up a black hose which he coiled onto the ground over sheets of black plastic where it was sunny and asked the new neighbors if we could rent water. They agreed. I forget how he rigged the sprayer head up in the air, but a kiddy pool made the base of the shower. He used tarps and towels draped over cloths line strung between trees to give a bit of privacy. The first girl of the morning got the hot shower. The other two suffered. Talk about shampoo sticky long hair!

Even the cats and dog had their places. Hobo had passed away just as we were clearing the lot and he was buried at one back edge of the lot. The new dog Andrew spent his time on a line snapped to the wooden dog house Sy had built in the past. The cats seemed to understand that this was a new home all but Puss who kept going back to the ugly green house. And the new owners would stop by to ask if we would please come and collect our cat.

We spent the summer camping out behind our house-in-construction and fortunately none of the neighbors turned us in. The girls flirted with the construction workers much to my embarrassment but that is feminine energy in the early teens. I don't remember how I handled clients at that time. Maybe I took the summer off.

When September came, life in camp was getting very old and cold and the girls were beginning to grumble since they now had to get up in the wee hours of darkness to be off to high school. Ben stepped forward and offered us his lakeside cottage on the other edge of town. It was like heaven those last two or three weeks we spent in a real house.

I didn't tell you before that when Sy and I married and moved into the ugly green house, we came with four cats and a dog—he came with two cats, Casey and Impy, and two girls. I came with two cats, Puss and Footsie, Hobo the dog—and three girls. While we were still living in the ugly green house Casey wandered down onto the lake-side road, in Nerme, which is very narrow and did not make it to the new house. I have a very clear memory of walking along that narrow road, cars whizzing by us, behind Cora as she carried her precious lifeless cat back to the ugly green house where her father and the rest of the family held a funeral for Casey.

The other sad story is that living in a woodsy environment all summer long I lost one of my engagement earrings. I was broken hearted and Sy spent many long hours walking the property to see if he could find it. He was good at that sort of endeavor. Twigs make an awfully good camouflage for an amethyst stone. We never did find the earring. Sy consoled me with the fact that once we were settled in the new house we would go back to Daniel who had made our wedding rings and have him design a ring with the remaining stone that would fit with my wedding band. I felt a bit better.

I don't remember the actual move into our new home, maybe because we moved from a camp site, then a summer cottage, and also storage places, rather than taking things off a moving truck and placing them in the new home.

I could bore you with the many happy memories that took place in that space we called Lakeview. It was in that kitchen where Sy thumped the red kitchen counter and said that in a hundred years we wouldn't remember what we were fighting about.

BOYFRIENDS

Chapter Twenty-Eight

Boyfriends for the girls had already entered our lives before we left the 'ugly green house.' Cora tended to have many male friends over the years before she married. One of the first came from the Thames City area while she was still living at home with us. This particular gentleman had come to spend the day with her and as the day lapsed into late afternoon and then evening, she came and asked if he could stay the night since he had no way to get home except for us to drive him—'and he lived a long ways away.' Sy and I looked at each other for a moment, both thinking 'how can we do this with a whole second floor of girls vulnerable to a young man prowling in the night.' Sy did a, "Cora, your step-mother and I have to talk about this first before we can give you an answer." That seemed to satisfy her for the moment.

In Sy's typical fashion he turned to me and said, "So what do you think we should do? This subject is going to come up again if we no bid it now."

"I agree." I responded. "But where can we bed him down for the night so that everyone is safe?"

"Well, that was my question to you," Sy said.

At that moment I had a flash of brilliance. Our garage stood on the basement level of the house and you had to come up an interior flight of stairs in the garage to a landing and then enter the kitchen. For some reason the builder had extended this landing, about four feet wide, all the way forward to the front of the garage. We used it as a storage area to stash those things we couldn't find space for in the main house. "What if we cleared off that platform got him an air mattress, a sleeping bag, and a pillow? That should make a neat private bedroom for him even if he has to share space with the cars down below. And we'd hear the kitchen door open if there were to be any shenanigans in the night."

"I'll give him a flash light so that he can see in the dark," Sy added.

The plan was struck and we set about clearing out the landing. Cora came to us later for the answer to her question and we told her that her boyfriend could stay.

"So where are you going to put him?" she asked.

"Come," I said, leading her to the garage. "We've made a nice bed for him here," I said as I pointed to the landing with the sleeping bag and pillow.

"You're putting him here?!" She asked.

"We thought it was a cozy spot," I responded.

As far as I can remember, we never had another male overnight guest.

Elizabeth was shy and quiet and somewhat to herself as a girl. But one spring morning during her junior year of high school, I looked out our kitchen window to see a blue, older-model car purring in our driveway. "Hey, Elizabeth," I called up the stairs. "What is that car doing in our driveway with the engine running?" I'm not sure how I knew the car was related to her, but then I am a mother.

"That's Jon," she called back. "He's going to take me to school this morning."

"Oh, no, he's not taking you to school in his car," I said. My mind flashed back to my high school years and all the girls who did not ride the school bus with me, but rode to school in boyfriends' cars. Some never got to school, and later, some had to drop out of school because of what went on in that car–on the way to school.

"No, he is not taking you to school in his car," I said. "In fact, you are going to go out there and tell him that you can't go to school with him in his car."

The look of defiance on her face would have stopped a grizzle bear, as the tears started to slide down her cheeks. I felt terrible but I believed I needed to protect my daughter until we knew Jon better.

"I'll go tell him," I said. And I can still feel the cool dew on the side of his car as I stood, elbows in the moisture, and leaned toward him to tell him that Elizabeth could not ride to school with him.

He very politely said, "Oh, I didn't know. She didn't tell me." Putting his car into reverse, he almost spun out of the driveway.

I think it took more than a week for Elizabeth to forgive me. I tried to explain why I had said no—but at that age there is no logical explanation. We did get to know Jon because over time he became a regular at our house. He was quiet, polite and he seemed to understand Elizabeth perhaps better than we did. They went together through the rest of her high school years. And my guess is that by senior year she was riding to school with him—with or without permission.

Towards the end of her being in the home before going off to college, Sy came to me one day and said, "Are you aware of the large mound of beer cans back in the woods?" I assured him I was unaware but we both had wondered if Elizabeth had developed a drinking problem. Even before Jon, she had come home late from an evening out with a new girlfriend; this was unusual for Elizabeth. She walked back to the family room and hung on the door frame with no apology to us for being late. Her words seemed slurred when she said she'd had fun and then told us she needed to get to bed. We both wondered if this new friend was leading her in an unfavorable direction, but, as is often true for parents, I didn't want to investigate the subject since it had taken her so long to find a friend. Sy as a step-father didn't want to stir things up for me.

Fast forward a bit. It was now time for Elizabeth to be going off to college. She begged us to let her forget about college even though she had been accepted at the Junior College in Bunker City. I said, "No. You think that Jon is all that you need. And he may be the right one for you, but if he is the man for you, he will wait until your two years are done in Bunker City." We went around and around the subject, but I stayed firm. She did ride up to school with him that first day as you've already read and I'm sure her good byes to him were even more tearful than the ones with me.

Sometime in her senior year of college she came home unannounced, not even coming to our home, and found Jon with someone else. I don't know where she stayed that weekend for she didn't tell me until much later about what she had found.

After college graduation Elizabeth returned home to us. During that summer Jon was back and asking her to come and live at his family home while he broke ground behind his parent's home in order to build a house for he and Elizabeth. She did go and stayed a month or so in his parental home. Elizabeth, like her mother, was out there in the woods helping him to clear the land when she was bitten by a Lyme tick. She showed me the spot a few days later and we got her to medical assistance quickly. She didn't seem very sick, but somehow during that time, she decided that living right behind his family home would be too confining for her and she seemed to break it off with Jon.

Felicia started around age fourteen to be interested in a boy that lived down the street from the new house we had just built. She spent much time going to hang out outside his house, but I'm not sure they ever made a true connection.

Life really began a few years later when Felicia was a junior in high school. I was driving her somewhere up route twelve when she suddenly pointed to a vehicle going by and said, "Mom, that's his truck!"

"Whose truck?" I asked

"His truck. That's his truck!"

"Does this His have a name?" I asked her.

She looked at me as if she thought I was stupid and said, "That's Joe's truck!" And in that moment a mother knows—this is the soul mate. We saw a lot of Joe, which was fine, for we both liked him. He seemed clean cut with a mischievous streak. My daughter wouldn't have wanted anything else. Joe was connected with the fire house in Sanford and his folks lived in Sanford, Connecticut. The two dated through the rest of her junior year and he took her to her prom--both junior and senior years--with the pretty prom dresses, flowers and photographs. Senior year saw them as a regular item.

Felicia wanted a car, so Sy and I went with her until we found a gray, sleek-looking car that we could afford. She put a down payment on it and then the problem arose that she was not eighteen yet which meant she could not have ownership. We didn't want to take on another car, so we three talked to Joe to see if he would take ownership of the car and then, when she turned eighteen, she would buy it from him for a dollar. He agreed and she was delighted.

Well, by the time she turned eighteen, he wouldn't give it back or sell it to her. We were horrified, because, up to that point, we hadn't seen this side of Joe. I'm not sure what Sy threatened, but Joe did eventually give over ownership and we wondered if we had misjudged him to begin with.

In the early spring of Felicia's senior year in high school she came to me and said that she was having trouble holding Joe off sexually and wanted to go on birth control pills. I was busy with work and I'm not sure what had me so consumed mentally, but I told her in June I would take her to a doctor to get her birth control pills. It wasn't too much later when she came to me and told me that she and Joe were getting engaged. It seemed a little early in their lives but you could see that they really appeared to be meant for each other. The ring arrived and his parents put on a little engagement party at their home in Sanford. At the time I was surprised that his parents didn't seem very happy about the engagement. They seemed a bit standoffish. But we didn't know them very well at that time.

*Felicia and Joe at Christmas
Before their Engagement*

I don't think Felicia wanted to, but she finished her senior year and graduated along with the other students. She and Joe continued to date, but you could feel there was a strain. This particular evening, Joe was having supper along with us in the kitchen of the new house and Elizabeth was there with a girl friend of hers. At some point I looked up to see that Joe and Elizabeth's girl friend were flirting silently across the table. Felicia never saw it.

Time came to take Felicia off to college and we once again carried all her gear in our wagon while she rode with Joe so that he could see where her room would be. Felicia has never been as outwardly affectionate with me as her sister Elizabeth, so she was sitting, curled up on her bed, when it was time to say good bye. She looked so forlorn as I hugged her and turned to leave. I knew Joe would be there for a while longer and then she would be into her new life. It was hard for me to leave her.

As time moved on that year Felicia reported that Joe didn't write much and that he seemed distant. He would come to see her when she came home but you could feel something was missing. She announced that she was coming home at the end of the first semester with plans to go to a local college for her second semester. I can't remember if that ever happened, but she did come home. I began to do some spy work and suggested that when she was up for it, she needed to check Elizabeth's friend's apartment complex.

She told me I was crazy for a long while, but then she did go and look and found Joe's truck in the parking lot. She confronted him and broke the engagement. After that Felicia spiraled down into a dark place for a long time.

Annie did not seem to care much about the boys other than a silent crush on a boy who had lived on the same street as she when she was a little girl. In high school I don't remember hearing about any boys and we thought it was because she always seemed a little younger than the other girls. I understand from Felicia who, ultimately, wound up going to the same college as Annie, (on a second try for both of them) that Annie was a bit more interested in boys by then. Obviously I wasn't in the loop at that time.

There is more love life for all of these girls, but that comes later.

THE BOOK STORE

Chapter Twenty-Nine

In and around the adventures of the girls, Sy and I were still working our jobs outside the home. I was counseling one day a week in the Medfield Pastoral Center and maintaining a small, private counseling practice at home in Nerme. I had been invited to join a professional group of other counselors, some psychological and some what we call 'body workers' who work with moving energy through the body to bring about healing. We held our meetings once a month in the Center Town Federated Church since it was the most central location for most of us. We shared our work, what we were reading, and any new workshops that we attended. And of course, there was sisterly support for those things going on in our private lives.

    The leader, Jenny, started talking about a book she was reading and the surprise was that three of us were also reading the same book—"Joy's Way" by W. Brugh Joy, M.D. I believe this book was the force that opened my life and living to a new way of thinking about the world around me. It was written by a doctor who was experimenting with the light he was seeing around his hands. As he touched patients, he discovered that those areas on their bodies that he had touched seemed to improve. He then started touching with the intent of healing the body and was amazed at the result.

    It was about a month after our book discussion, when one of the women in the group, a minister's wife, told us that she had just had a second check up with her doctor and he had told her that she had so many cysts on both ovaries that she would be unable to have children. We commiserated with her and then Jenny said, "What are we doing?

You--meaning the minister's wife--go lie down on that couch over there and the rest of us will put our hands on you."

I remember being down on my knees on the floor beside Jenny saying, "Do you know what we're doing?"

And she responded, "No, but it feels right."

A month later our friend was back at the meeting and she said, "I have an announcement to make."

We were curious.

"The doctor checked me over two days ago and he couldn't believe what he saw. The cysts are all gone." He said, "I'd advise you to go home and get pregnant quickly because I don't know what you did and I don't know how long it will last." She had her first child ten months later.

In a little less than a year she came to us again and said, "I want another child and the cysts are back. Can you fix me?"

We put her back on the couch and worked on her again. The energy in the room was almost enough to make you reel. She went on to have her second child.

I was traveling from Nerme to Center Town to attend these meetings and this particular day was a brilliantly sunny, warm day. I can remember feeling really great and day-dreaming as I drove. Suddenly I thought, 'I'm going to open a book store.' And in the next space, I thought, 'Where did that notion come from?' I mulled the message over in my mind, and by the time I got to the meeting, I could hardly wait to tell my group. The first moment when I had their attention I said, "I'm going to open a book store!"

"Hey, that's a great idea," one of them responded.

And another said, "Do you know anything about running a book store?"

I had to answer, "No, but that's what I'm going to do." Living as long as I have now, I know my guides were telling me to open the store, because anything that comes from that far outside your normal thought pattern is a message from your guides—or for some—from God.

I went home that day and continued to ponder the whole idea and then how was I going to present this to Sy? When our coffee time came, I chose to present it as something that had happened to me on the way to my meeting.

He was dumb-founded and asked the same question. "Do you know anything about running a book store or any store for that matter?"

I had to confess that I didn't know any more than he did and that I would need his help. I had been on the computer that afternoon and was looking for workshops or places where we could get training on such an endeavor. The American Book Sellers Association was doing a weekend workshop in Campbell, Massachusetts for people wanting to open a book store and it was that coming weekend. We would have to make our reservation in the next two days to be able to attend. We didn't even have enough money in our bank account to cover the cost, but I had a little counseling money left for that month and that's what we went on.

Even at the conference, people would ask why we were attending and we'd both answer, "We're not sure, but we are supposed to open a book store."

Fast forward to a mini vacation we took to Vermont a short while after the conference. On the long drive home I was musing about the store front that I had found in a reasonable location in the Flowers section of Nerme, Connecticut.

Sy's voice broke the silence as he said, "What if we call our store Merlin Books?"

"That's perfect," I responded. With that comment from Sy, I knew that he was on board, if not a bit reluctantly.

We soon procured a lease on the store front, hired a local artist to develop a logo, and set about preparing the interior space to become a book store. Sy built all of the adjustable book shelves and later the roll-about book and gift display pieces. Together we painted the store in a soft blue because Merlin, in the logo form, was done in a deep blue—the color that one sees in healing work when the wound is beginning to close. The shelves were left natural and I have a very clear memory of being down on the floor in the empty store in May, the store door open to the spring breezes, while I painted layers of polyurethane onto those unassembled book shelves. The music playing in the back ground was the bouncy music of 'Deep Breakfast' by Ray Lynch, which, to some extent became our theme song.

We enlisted friends to help and the day dawned on the first Friday in June for the opening. I remember that it was frantic getting everything ready and in place. There were refreshments and a door prize. As people came in, more and more, I did as I so often do when I'm overwhelm—I became somewhat disassociated. Neither of us was prepared for the great number of people who came to the opening.

First night turned into week days working in the store ordering books and meeting representatives of different book companies who were trying to get you to carry their books. Within the first month I found that I had no connection to the bestselling books of the day and I was having trouble ordering what we needed. I talked with Sy and said, "I need to turn this store into a metaphysical book store. There is none in this area and I can't seem to connect with conventional books."

So with his support we switch our merchandise. It soon became apparent that we needed more to draw people in. I began to set up workshops to teach some of the subjects that were in the books people were buying.

I had hired an astrologer that I had taken classes from at a previous time and he taught for us for a year, but his classes didn't draw enough people to continue. About this time, a good looking, older gentleman, with a shock of white hair, came into the store and asked if we needed any more help. I told him that my classes were set up and 'no' I didn't need anyone else. He seemed reluctant to leave and then he said that he could do intuitive readings for us. I still dismissed him. When I went home, I couldn't get this man out of my mind. I went back and forth on how I could use this person in the store. Two days later I contacted him and asked him to come and read for me. He did. At first I didn't connect with what he was telling me about my future until he described Grampa Joe down to the glasses and personality. I hired Whitley and he became the back bone of our store, teaching courses on metaphysics—intuitive reading, past lives, meditation, distance vision and many more subjects.

I found that my natural shyness vanished as I was selling merchandise. I loved being with the people on a day-to-day basis and working with sales people who came to sell us rocks and teach us how to use stones for healing. Then I had to learn about jewelry and find a jeweler who could make one-of-a-kind items for the display case someone had given us. Business was good and people were buying.

At one point, Sy and I had to go for my annual appointment with my gynecologist in Bunker City, over a hundred miles away, while helpers ran the store. We were in a restaurant in Dawns Town, Massachusetts, just outside Bunker City when I heard the people in the booth behind me talking.

"Have you been to that new book store in Nerme, Connecticut? It's just off the highway." I heard one say. I couldn't believe my ears, so leaned in a bit. "No, but I've heard it is a really nice space. Nice energy. They teach there and you can find products that we can't get around here." I relayed what I was hearing to Sy and he just smirked, I think with pride.

We had been running the store for about a year with the help of two friends who were now employees. Ginger had heard of a woman psychic in the area who was very good and wanted time off to go for a reading with this person. When she came back she stepped inside the front door, closed it, and said, "The psychic says to tell you that you are very sick with something."

My response was, "I'm fine and she is crazy." But I listened to what Ginger had been told about her own life and it made sense. By the next month I wasn't feeling well so I made an appointment with this same woman.

When I finally walked into her reading room her first words were, "Who is that feisty little old lady trailing along behind you? --That lady with the gray bun on her head. She's not very tall." There was only one person it could be—and I responded, "That's my grandmother." Then the psychic tried to get my grandmother's name. Mary came easily but she had trouble and started," Em...Emily...no, something that starts with an E."

I said, "Her name is Mary Emma Moody."

"That's right Mary Emma," she replied, the way my grandmother always referred to herself.

The outcome of the interview was that I had something that was making me sick and sapping my energy and I should get myself to a doctor soon. I didn't do anything for a bit as I pondered what it could be and then I remembered a conversation I'd overheard at a workshop I had attended the year before on Past Life Regression.

It was noontime and we students were taking our lunch in the dining hall. A woman at my table was talking about the strange disease she had been wrestling with for the past year. Each doctor that she went to prescribed something different, which seemed to work at first and then made her worse. She said, "When I finally found myself crawling to the toilet and back again to my bed, I decided to stop all medication and see a Naturopathic doctor. She put me on various herbs, an exercise program, meditation, and I'm strong enough now to attend this workshop."

I went to Sy with this remembered conversation and he said, "We had a Naturopathic doctor in here about a month ago to do a workshop. Why don't you go see her?"

I called, made my appointment, liked her very much, and Desire McDonald ordered all sorts of tests, telling me that we had to rule out a lot of things before we could proceed. I went through that process, and when the day came for the verdict, she told me I had Chronic Fatigue and she wanted me to take this homeopathic on my way home. I can remember putting the little white pellets under my tongue. By the time I got to the Cold Star Bridge heading towards Nerme, the fog in my brain began to lift and I suddenly became aware of the cars to my right and left. Up to that point I hadn't been seeing or thinking clearly and hadn't recognize the loss of cognitive function.

Over time I got better, but I began to have trouble when someone would call and ask if we had a certain book on the shelf. I'd hear the title, put the telephone down, walk across the room and I couldn't remember the title. After a lot of this type of embarrassment, Sy and I decided that we needed to hire a manager to help in the store. With all the synchronicity that circled around that store, a church friend came into the shop a few days later and told us her daughter was home and looking for work. We hired Norina and she became my extra brain. She was gracious, dependable and pretty to look at.

We had reached our fifth year in the store—the magic number for success or failure—and were headed into the recession of 1989 and 1990. A metaphysical book store had opened in Mystand two towns away. A conventional book store had opened in the other end of Nerme and that store was using computers while we were still doing orders by hand.

We had many large crystals around the store on display, one of which sat near the front of the store. Grampa Joe had given this to us as we opened the store. One day when Whitley came to work, he stopped to hold it and almost fell over. He started telling us about a civilization that I suppose was part of South America in earlier times. He quickly put it back and said that no one should bother that stone.

Close to the ending of Merlin Books, a group of high school boys came into the store and stole almost all those displayed crystals including the powerful one up front. Norina went to work, contacted the high school principal, and told him we needed those crystals back with no questions asked. Within two weeks they were all back except the sacred one in the front of the store. From the time that crystal disappeared our sales began to drop off. I have often wondered what happened to the person who took it and where it is now.

Sy and I finally had to come to terms with the fact that we either had to sell the store or close it down. I couldn't hear him for a while and we went back into therapy. With the help of the therapist I came to terms with the fact that no matter how happy I was in the store, it was going to start eating away at our personal finances. We put the store up for sale and couldn't find anyone who wanted to put in seventy to eighty hours a week running a store. Merlin Books closed in the fall of 1991 with Norina overseeing the bulk of the selloff.

Our customers were wonderful, coming and buying books I'm sure they didn't need to help us through that sad period. It was so painful for me that we took a trip through the Southwest while the buy down was taking place. Norina did a superb job of clearing the store and getting as much as she could financially to clear any debts.

TRANSITIONS

Chapter Thirty

Sy had been talking to Grampa Joe and he was encouraging Grampa Joe to come to live in Nerme in the Morrison House an old hotel on Main Street that rents rooms by the week, month or year. Many elderly people have finished their time at the Morrison House. Grampa Joe was talking about how lonely he was and how much up-keep there was for one person in his little red house. Sy reported this conversation to me and we thought it would be delightful to have Grampa Joe close enough that he could enjoy the grandchildren before they were all grown and into their personal lives or married. Next we heard that he was packing things, giving items away, and having the Salvation Army come to clean up the rest. That sounded reasonable and we continued on with our plans to start Merlin Books.

We were about two weeks into our new book store being open for business, when Grampa Joe knocked at our door and came in. He sat down in the rocker and said, "Well, it's all gone, all but my personal things. The house is sold and now I'm here."

Sy said, "What did the Morrison House say about a room?"

"I haven't asked them yet."

Sy's voice lifted a bit and he said, "What do you mean you haven't asked them, yet?"

"Well, I was busy getting things packed and I didn't think much about that."

"Okay, so where are you planning on staying tonight and then next week?" Grampa Joe looked like he'd just been run over by a truck and he mumbled something.

"When we suggested you come to Nerme, it was to live on Main Street. We don't have an extra room here and you didn't tell us that you intended to come to Nerme, so we went ahead and started this book store."

At that point I'm not sure who looked the most disgruntled, Grampa Joe or Sy. Grampa heaved himself up out of his chair and said, "Well you don't have to worry about me. I'll find a place! I've always survived."

We were on our way to the store when Grampa Joe arrived and we felt we had to continue on with the project of running the store, never having heard that Joe was taking us up on Sy's suggestion. I agonized, and as the days passed and we didn't see Grampa Joe, we began to be concerned. About four days later he re-emerged in better spirits and said he had been eating a meal in town and this lovely woman came in. He struck up a conversation with her. She was in need of a boarder and he needed a place to live. As luck would have it, she lived just around the corner from our house. Grampa Joe spent several years there but came less and less to visit with the girls as they were growing into their own lives and his world was getting smaller. He finally had to move to a Gentlemen's Home in Whaling City; an older home devoted, at that time, to the needs of aging men run by a lovely, compassionate, attentive woman as house mother.

Felicia graduated from high school in 1987 and Annie graduated in 1988. Annie had been held back in first grade because her parents and teacher felt she was not mature enough to handle the second grade work. That being the case, Felicia had gone off to her Junior College in the fall before Annie graduated from high school. Annie, her father, and I went to visit Damon Junior College in Frisco, Massachusetts. She had her interview and we three were charmed by the small school atmosphere. She was accepted and Sy and I loaded her into our wagon along with enough stuff to last for two years, I swear, and an over large dog I had gotten for her bed. I had had such a friend when I started college.

Annie lasted about three days and the telephone rang. Sy was always the one to answer the phone in our house so I had to listen to his end of the conversation. She hated the school, was lost, and homesick. She wanted to come home. "Okay I'll come get you," Sy said. I was livid because I knew from my own experience of going off to college that she could make it. She just would have to suffer through the initial pain.

Annie came home. Now we had two daughters floating around with no sense of direction while we were too busy to give direction. Felicia did get a job and I guess Annie baby sat or maybe she also got a job. The part that was disturbing both of us was that Felicia was socializing at night in an area of Thames City that was most unsavory and she wasn't aware or didn't care. By spring both Sy and I had had enough of these aimless daughters, so we called them together, sat them down at that trestle table in the kitchen and said, "Starting next week we are going to ask you to pay us $80.00 dollars a week for room and board and you will be taking your laundry to the town laundromat."

I could see Felicia's wheels turning and suddenly she said, "I think I'll go back to school. Maybe I can go to Damon College. Mom, you said they had a good music program there?"

Surprised but not unhappy I said, "Yes, they have a very good music program. And Annie, if your sister is going to Damon, do you think you could go back with her and the two of you manage to get through your two years, together?"

Annie looked a bit contemplative and then said, "Yes, with Felicia there I could do it."

The plan was made and they both went off to Damon Junior College that coming fall. Would you believe, they don't look anything alike, two different fathers were paying the bills, and the administrators managed to put the two of them together in the same small house of only seven rooms? I don't think the school figured out for some time that they were sisters coming from the same household. I'm sure they didn't function as friends but they still held each other up through those two years. Annie wound up having to graduate at a different time than Felicia, and at the moment, I don't remember the circumstances. Felicia emerged with a degree in music and discovered that she did, indeed, have quite a voice. Annie got her degree in child care, a place where she is a natural.

Elizabeth was through college and was coming to the end of her free year at home. She apparently panicked and we came home from the store one day to find her room stripped of everything except the furniture and Elizabeth gone. No note, no phone call, nothing. I was beside myself, but by now I had learned to give the girls space to give us an explanation. After a tortuous week I cornered Felicia and asked, "Where is your sister?"

"I think she moved over the other side of town with Miles.

"Well, is she planning on coming home or when was she contemplating on telling us?"

"I don't know but I believe she is living with Miles," Felicia responded.

It took a while but gradually Elizabeth came to visit. Miles was a lot like her father—devil may care, life of the party--and knowing how I felt about a partner like that I think, she was afraid I would disapprove. The best way around that was not to tell me anything. We received an invitation to come and inspect their apartment and I felt much better. Elizabeth and Miles did indeed have a lovely little place close to where Sy had originally lived.

The two lived together for some time; they even moved together to an apartment in Grows Town, which put him closer to his work as a young man who laid household and commercial carpet. They were not in Grows Town for very long, just long enough to acquire two dogs. We got a frantic call from Elizabeth one evening that she had to come home again and would we mind if she brought one of the dogs. As loving parents we went to collect her, some of her things, and Jake, the boisterous dog. There had been a bad fight and we got no details that were coherent.

This time I gave Elizabeth four months to get herself reorganized and then she needed to find a place for herself. Once again, time was getting short and she seemed to not be taking any steps to move forward. We came home from the store one day to find that Jake was gone. I was concerned and I think it was Annie who blurted out, "Elizabeth called the vet this morning and took Jake to be put down. She knew she couldn't find any place that would take him. She dug a big hole in the way back yard and he's out there." --Oh, how I wish Elizabeth could have communicated with us!

It was shortly after that when in the evening Miles appeared at our front door in tears. He wanted Elizabeth back and she wouldn't answer his calls. Could we intervene to let her know he'd changed and he needed her back. I was convinced he was sincere and so we talked with Elizabeth. Not long after those conversations, Elizabeth announced that she was engaged to Miles and they were planning a wedding in September of 1990.

Cora had been out on her own through all of her sister's adventures, living in different apartments and with different gentlemen friends. She had been home for Christmas and was frighteningly thin for her frame. I talked with her and she seemed in good spirits but a little on edge. I have a picture taken that Christmas that shows her hands, and for a therapist, I could see she was playing with her food. When I confronted her, she denied it, but told me her new friend didn't want her to get fat and so she was watching her diet closely. The more she talked about this young man, the more fearful I became, but at that age a young woman doesn't listen to her mother.

Sometime after that conversation, Cora called and asked to speak to her father. That was not unusual because the girls had already learned that I was likely to say 'no' and he would say 'yes.' I didn't think much about it. When he was done talking he turned to me and his face was drained. "Cora is pregnant and needs a trip to the abortion clinic. Her friend wants no part of this situation, so she is alone. She needs me to take her in tomorrow."

"Oh, Honey, I'm so sorry. Should I go with you?"

"No, I need to do this with her by myself."

He spent the next day with Cora, got her home to her apartment and into bed and cozied her up as much as he could. Sy returned home quiet and only willing to give me the brief details for he was in mourning for a lost grandchild and for a daughter he could not really help. When she was able to talk with both of us, she told me that she felt she had lost a pair of twins making it doubly difficult to recover.

My time line is a little bent this many years later, but it was not too much later when a new man appeared in Cora's life who came from Nerme. A relative of his lived just down the road from us and somehow that made him a better candidate than many of the others she had dated. This new man, Donald, became a regular when we saw Cora and he came to Christmas along with the rest of the family. Cora and Don found an apartment in Whaling City and settled into domestic life. She called and invited us to come see their new apartment and to have dinner with them. This felt so good and normal. We heaved a sigh of relief and said we'd come.

Dinner was pleasant and Donald did his best to be the good host and keep Cora on track in the kitchen. We left them feeling that things were going to work out for Cora. Sometime in the night we were awakened by a frantic telephone call from Don, "I don't know what's happened to Cora, but she's just pierced the cats' ears and put stud earrings into their ears. I can't get her to come to bed. She's nuts!"

I could hear Sy with his ever present calm, "Try to get her to bed, Don. Give her something like warm milk to calm her down and we will be there in the morning." I'm not sure if Sy slept at all that night. In the early hours of the morning we had a call from the police that they had picked up a blonde on the edge of Rhode Island in her car, which was up against the guardrail. When they asked her how she'd gotten there, she couldn't remember. But she did have information with her and Sy was the contact person. Where did he want them to take her? Without skipping a beat, Sy responded, "Take her to the BC&C Hospital Psychiatric Ward. I'll be there as soon as I can."

I had to go to work at the store while Sy went to the hospital. Afterwards he told me that he and the doctors went around and around as to what could be the problem for Cora, and Sy finally said, "I believe it is Bipolar Disorder. Her mother was never diagnosed but she was better when she could get her hands on Lithium." Treatment was started immediately and Cora began to recover.

All the time Cora was in the hospital, Don was there every day at some point to talk with her, get what he could for her, read the newspaper to her and generally be attentive, while working and taking care of their apartment. Bipolars can be very demanding, self-concerned and unaware of others, especially while they are going through an episode. Donald weathered all of it with a smile. Ultimately we were feeling much better about Cora's future.

I could go on with all the little details, but down the road Cora decided that Don was not for her, because in her eyes, he was immature and she didn't feel completely safe with him. Cora spent time alone in apartments in Thames City as she recovered and came to grips with having a lifelong disease.

It was when Annie was graduated from college and back home for her year of preparing for independence that she reconnected with a high school friend, Shawn, who now wanted to be more than a friend. They were both computer people and connected around working with computers. Things grew to the place where they were talking about marriage, and short of setting a firm date, she and I talked about me making the dress and just what it would look like. Annie began gathering paper products and the two of us went and picked out the pattern for her wedding dress: the cloth, netting, and all the adornments.

Shawn had enlisted with the Army and was sent to Texas. He invited Annie to follow him. She debated, discussed it with us, and then decided to drive that long distance in her new car. I forget how long they were together in Texas when we got the call that she had been in a car accident and nearly totaled her car. Shawn wasn't being much help, and somehow, she needed to come home. Sy quietly suggested that she had gotten herself into this situation and needed to find a way home herself. Ultimately her friend did help getting her and the car home, but by then the romance was gone and I had a closet full of fabrics which I kept for many years. At a later date Annie got word that her friend had died suddenly in a car crash, but the details were hazy.

Annie had more than one job, some in child care and then in other things over the next years, and moved to at least two apartments. She was in Thames City when she lost her job, had just purchased some large computer equipment and now was going to have to leave her apartment. She opened the door, let the cat go, and then called asking us if she could come home. I think by now Sy had had enough of wandering daughters and said no, that we didn't have any spare room for her. My heart ached for her but he was right; we didn't have extra space. We had just moved into a Senior Community with no thought of housing returning daughters. A few days later she called to tell us that Steven was going to let her stay with him in Newburg. Could we please come and help her move all of her stuff? We did—car loads of clothes, equipment, and you name it, not to mention her bird. Even Steven was forced into a car run or two. It was during that event that we met Steven, a young man from Europe, working in some sort of construction, we thought.

You guessed it--the weddings are coming.

Dressed for Felicia's First Wedding
Cora, Sy, and Annie Standing Together in the Pool Room of Lakeview

LETTING GO FOR THE NEW

Chapter Thirty-One

As Merlin Books closed, I retreated to my home and home office to regroup. My friend Ginger had started joining me to do body work on my clients that seemed stuck in their process. We worked together in my office above the house garage. As things evolved we started talking about establishing a little counseling center with her and another friend Linda, both the old employees from the store. Linda also did body work. As we talked and included her in these discussions we became Abintra Counseling. My office space, though large, was too small for all of us to work together. I came up with the idea to put a dormer on the garage of our home at Lakeview, which would enlarge it enough to include two more counseling rooms and a waiting room. Ginger's significant other was an independent builder and we asked if he would be willing to do the plans and the construction. He agreed and we went through the process of enlarging our counseling rooms. It was a magnificent, cozy space and we three settled into that comfortable environment.

I don't know what possessed me or how long it took before I decided that the whole establishment on Lakeview was too large for us to maintain. I am a garden person and have a habit of designing and then building the gardens around a house until they are larger than I can maintain. And I had done that at Lakeview, then realizing that all of our girls were now off and into their own lives. I brought my concerns to Sy and he said, "Well, I guess that means we need to put this house up for sale and find a smaller place."

I responded with, "So what do we do with the business?"

"It looks like you will have to find a new location."

As this was transpiring, a woman, who had been a regular in the Merlin Books classes and had become a close friend, was getting close to her next adventure. Hanna had signed up to go to the Barbara Brennen School of Energy Healing in Florida. We invited her to join us as she got her training. I believe it was she who found an office complex on Main Street, in Nerme Village, that we could all afford. I'm not sure why the move was rushed but it was and we painted, moved furniture and settled into Abintra Alternative Counseling Center on Main Street in one weekend.

Once again we put the house up for sale and it sold out from under us. We then also had to find a new place to live. Sy and I had been looking for an empty-nesters home in Nerme and the surrounding towns. Nothing spoke to us. Then, Sy saw an ad in the Whaling City newspaper, our local newspaper, advertising an information night given by Ben the man who had built our house on Lakeview. We went and he was showing his plans for a Senior Community to be built in Nerme just outside the Village. We took home all the information; house plans, plot lay out, and began our contemplation. I remember it was still cold in the spring but we bundled up and went to walk the property. At one point I got to the top of a hill and said, "There, that is the place for our house!"

And Sy responded, "Are you sure? Are you sure that is the right place?"

I knew. "That spot right there where the brush is, that is where our new home should be built!"

Now, I cannot fathom how my Love had so much faith in me, but he went about contacting Ben and signing us up for our house. Meanwhile we still had to find a place to live and we began driving around town. Within two days we had found a small house on Pine Cone Street in the Spiritualists Retreat area of Nerme. There had been a summer camp at one time in that area and the houses were packed close together but once again I fell in love. We set an appointment with the man who was listed on the For Rent sign and he allowed us a tour. We both stepped into this 1920's cottage, somewhat musty from being near the water, and it felt like I was home. Sy turned around and walked out saying, "It's too small.

Back at Lakeview we argued back and forth, each presenting ways in which our personal view was correct. Sy was very much not convinced that we could make Pine Cone Street a home for however many months

A Bird and the Dragon: Their Love Story

it would take to build our retirement place. Finally he relented, we signed our contract, and I began asking to change the appliances. Sy pointed out that the owner wouldn't pay—it would be out of our pocket. I knew, but I also knew we could be quite happy for some time if my kitchen worked properly. What I didn't know was that we also were going to have Felicia's infant son to raise two days a week.

Things did work out. I took many pictures of our retirement house going up and finally it was finished. There was one other house that had been completed before ours, but the owner had not yet sold her original home, so we were the first people to move into Chapwell Hills in Nerme, Connecticut. The community was so new that the road up to our house had just been completed and there was a barrier across the road at the base of the hill that had to be moved each time we came and went.

In 1989 Sy retired with an early retirement from The Lab. The department threw him a large party with many gag gifts and some lovely serious gifts, like his watch. In the years before, a group of his friends had gotten together and formed a dining-out club which they called 'The Dog Night.' I'm not sure, but I think we wives were the dogs. Many of these people were there and Sy was very touched by all the verbal and ceremonial tributes he received. Unfortunately he would never let me put up the plagues he was given for his work and service. I never could understand his view point. He had earned these awards—why not display them?

Sy moved on to do consulting work for a private firm that supported the government programs and enjoyed it, but not as much as the work at The Lab. By the time we were building a house with Ben, Sy was near retirement again. He asked Ben if he could use help organizing the office at Chapwell Hills or any other details, and Ben hired him as the foreman. About a year after starting to live in our retirement house Sy was working about two doors down from us in the model home. A much better commute to work!!

A baby boy, you say and how did we get there? I have to go back and gather up some loose ends.

LOSE ENDS

Chapter Thirty-Two

Grampa Joe spent his last Christmas with us in 1988 and passed away some time after that. Because he had become a part of our extended family, all of the girls that were available went to his service in the same funeral home that had managed Gramma Bootsie's burial. When Min's mother died, Sy had collected his ex-wife alone and had had a hard time getting her past the bars because she kept asking to stop and get a drink. This time he suggested that we all ride with him to go pick up Min and take her to the service. When we got to the nursing home I assigned Felicia to sit in the front seat between Sy and Min, while I would sit in the back between Annie and Cora.

I believe Min stayed through the service this time. When we had gotten her back to the nursing home and it was just our family in the car Felicia said, "Mom, why the heck did you put me in the front seat between Sy and Min?"

"With you between them, they didn't fight and it was the same reason I sat in the back between Annie and Cora. Everyone was anxious and on edge and it avoided a whole bunch of unpleasantness," I responded.

"Oh," she replied. "It was very uncomfortable and I wondered."

When I met Sy, Mignon had left him for a man that was a great deal more like her father, Grampa Joe, and who was like she, an alcoholic. I have to assume there were happy moments, but he did beat her several times. Once she called and asked Sy to come and rescue her, but he told her this was a matter for the police and she should call them to ask for help. Min told the judge at Sy's divorce that she had met me and felt I would make a

A Bird and the Dragon: Their Love Story

very good mother for her children. I went to visit her shortly after Sy and I were married as a bit of an insurance policy to what might lie ahead of me with him as my partner. She was very polite and didn't really tell me much except to say that he had strong opinions and seemed to think that he was always right. For me that was not a problem for, when he was in that mode, he was usually correct. I had worked for years to build enough ego strength so that aspect of his personality didn't challenge me.

As time moved along, Min's living companion passed away and she went into a nursing home. On several occasions Cora and Annie were told by the nursing home staff that their mother was very ill. We would take the children to see her. I think she frightened Annie, for Annie would usually stay close to me and only speak when spoken to by her mother. Cora, on the other hand, visited her mother on her own and had a reasonable relationship with Min.

The day finally came when Cora was saying that she didn't think her mother was going to come back this time. A couple of days later the nursing home called and said they felt we should come so the girls could have their last visit. We brought Annie who was now out of college and Cora arrived by herself a short while later. Both girls positioned themselves on each side of Min's hospital bed as the woman labored for air. Cora was holding Min's hand and talking to her but again, Annie didn't know what to say. Min struggled to get oxygen, which was frightening to hear. I could see, standing at the end of the bed beside Sy, that something was keeping her from passing over. I suddenly remembered what a psychic had said to me years ago—"Annie has a contract with her mother. I don't know what it is about but they have a contract!" This seemed strange when she said it because when Min would come to collect the girls for a visit, she would sometimes forget to even get Annie.

I called softly to Annie, "Take your mother's hand. Tell her that you forgive her, that you love her, and that you and Cora will be alright." Annie looked at me for half a second, and then, turning back to her mother, she did as I suggested repeating what I had said. These were the words Min had needed, and in three minutes she was gone.

Cora made the burial arrangements, and since Min's parents had assumed Min would be buried with Sy, there was no burial plot for her. Cora found a single plot in a cemetery in Whaling City, Connecticut, and

Min was interred there. The girls never were able to find enough money for a stone marker and Sy didn't feel it was his place, so over time, I saved money out of my counseling income to purchase a very small stone marker. After all, Min was the mother of two of my daughters.

THE WEDDINGS

Chapter Thirty-Three

Before we get to the weddings, I need to give you some history. When I left Harvard, he did allow me to take the security funds that he had started for each daughter at their birth. I had told the girls that I wanted to oversee the fund until they were twenty-five, figuring that maybe by that age they might understand and pay attention to this money as a nest egg for their future. At age eighteen Elizabeth went to her father and told him that I wouldn't give them their money. Next thing I knew I had a letter in the mail from Harvard's lawyer stating that my holding the funds was illegal and if I didn't hand them over they would take court action. You can imagine that I was very angry but it was not worth a fight, so I handed over the accounts to both girls with the stipulation that I had planned to use a little of this money for their weddings. Since I was being forced to give the money to them at such an early age, they would be responsible for paying the costs of their own weddings.

Elizabeth was the first daughter to take the leap into the adult word of matrimony. Not long after she and Miles announced they were going to marry, Elizabeth came to me with the dress she had already purchased. It was a lovely lace over white, street-length dress with a Bolero Jacket that had the traditional long sleeves. She said, "I saw the dress and wanted it, so I went and bought it, but it is a little short. I'm not sure Miles will approve."

"Put it on," I suggested. "Let's take a look. Maybe it will be fine the way it is and maybe we'll have to work some magic."

Elizabeth went to put on her dress and reemerged in a lovely white wedding dress and oh, yes, a bit short.

"Honey," I said, "You are right. Miles will be upset at the length. But I think I have some lace in my sewing things that is the right quality for your beautiful dress." I did have lace, which I added to the bottom of the skirt making it appear like the trim of a slip. On her wedding day, wearing that dress, her brunette hair cascading down from under a brimmed hat, Elizabeth became a lovely, if nervous, bride.

Elizabeth and Miles made the trip to her father's house to ask if he would perform the ceremony since he was still a minister in a church. He agreed and they were married September 8, 1990, in the church where her father was the presiding minister. It is a lovely little church much like the one Harvard and I came to as pastor and new wife in Farmers, Connecticut. Since Elizabeth had asked me to walk her down the aisle, it left Sy with no official duty. Harvard asked him to stand at the front of the church and direct the people into their appropriate pews—bride's side, groom's side and then reverse it when the service was over.

Felicia was the maid-of-honor and once again, because I wasn't going to pay, we had to come up with something very inexpensive. By now all the girls wanted pretty dresses for the first wedding in our family. May had come home to witness her sister's big day. I took the girls to Sears and prayed all the way there that we could find something appropriate and inexpensive. They had a whole rack of various Calico flowered prints done up in peasant style dresses and we found ones to fit everyone in the party, including me. The girls used shoes they already owned. I know I did.

By the time we got to the flowers, I relented and Sy and I gave Elizabeth and Miles the flowers for their wedding.

It had been arranged that Felicia would sing a solo, but when it came time, she had too much stage fright and wouldn't share her talent with the audience.

One other event that wasn't expected was that my younger brother, Copeland brought a young woman as his guest. We all met Merrily Anne and really liked her. He was still single and in his early forties. At an earlier time, I had had a dream of a woman that would live above him in his apartment house who had children, but I knew they would not stand in the way of this union. The woman's name in the dream was Anne. As they were leaving the party, Copeland leaned toward me and whispered, "Merrily Anne was the closest I could find." They also went on to marry and some of our girls attended that wedding with us.

A Bird and the Dragon: Their Love Story

Because Elizabeth knew we were not going to provide her wedding, she and Miles asked his mother to handle the reception. With the help of some of their friends, his family put on a lovely garden reception at the back of their home. They had tied up a cluster of white bells on some birch trees in the yard, and since it was a warm sunny day, most of the photos were taken under the bells. Knowing Miles, I'm sure the party went on well into the night, but we left for home in the late afternoon to rest and regroup.

When life came back to normal, we were invited to see the house that would be their first home as married people. I was surprised that it was a summer cottage that was sort of fitted out for the winter, but not really. I think they nearly froze to death that first winter and were soon on to better living accommodations, but my heart sank at the thought that this cottage was all that Miles could afford for his new wife. And was this going to be her future?

One event I didn't mention is important to the connections that led Felicia to marry. When it came time to give Elizabeth a wedding shower, Felicia was not sure how to go about the affair. Cora had been living in an apartment in Whaling City that was an old house with several apartments. Sally, one of Cora's neighbors, and a new friend, offered her apartment as a place to hold the party. With the older two girls helping Felicia, she gave Elizabeth her bridal shower.

Through the next five years Felicia got to know Sally very well and was often invited to go on camping trips or picnics with Sally's family. At some point Sally began talking about her nephew that was about Felicia's age. He was of stocky build and good looking with some of that devil may care attitude of her father. Felicia was interested, and, even though Sally told her Chris was trouble, she still dated him. The first time we met Chris was at Thanksgiving in 1994. That is a hard time to bring a new person into the family, but he seemed to survive and they were married on September 18, 1995.

When it was time for the official engagement, Chris had to tell Felicia that he could not afford an engagement ring. She did not take it well. Sy listened in the back ground--as fathers often do--and in a short while I noticed he'd left the room. He came back with a ring box and a sapphire and diamond bracelet. "These were my mother's," he said to Felicia. "Look at the ring and see if the jeweler can create an engagement ring for you from my mother's jewelry. The jeweler made a lovely diamond ring with diamond chips on each side of the stone.

At the appropriate time, they too, went to Harvard and asked him to perform their marriage ceremony in his little church. This time Harvard said to Sy, "Since I can't be in two places at once and you have spent the bulk of these last years raising Felicia, why don't you walk her down the aisle." Felicia was delighted. She had grown used to Sy's steady ways and he would be a comfort in that high anxiety experience.

Felicia invited her new mother-in-law to be, Sandra, and I to go with her while she bought her wedding dress at a discount store in Medfield, Connecticut. Felicia had trouble deciding on her dress while we mothers found our dresses quickly. We did return triumphant from that trip. Felicia's dress was full length with lace overlay down the front and a lace stand-up collar and long traditional sleeves.

This time I offered to provide Felicia's flowers and a friend of Miles's who had a flower shop did all the flowers for us. Felicia's bouquet was a beautiful cascade of flowers which she carried as the final touches to her lovely white dress. The shoulder length toil veil enhanced the picture. The best photograph I have of Sy was taken standing next to Felicia as she displayed her wedding gown.

For Felicia's wedding, it was the rehearsal the evening before that created some of the drama. Everyone was excited and would not pay attention to Harvard's directions or quiet down enough so he could be heard. At one point he yelled at all of us and then got cooperation. Chris's father, Lance, and step-mother, Lisbeth, came and his mother and brother Scottie were there. Scottie was Chris's best man.

Felicia and Chris had a gloriously sunny wedding day and while we were occupied at the church, Chris's soon-to-be step-father was busy getting together the feast for the wedding guests. The reception was held in Nerme in our town Community Room. The meal was slow to be served, so there was dancing, and at one point, I stepped out of the ball room to find Chris. His bride was sitting at the head table with her sister Elizabeth and no one else. I saw him in the parking lot smoking with his friends and I wondered if this was a picture of the future. Felicia reported that it was one of the happiest days of her life. That's all any mother wants to hear.

Cora had been living in an apartment building in Thames City and began talking about a young man around her age that was living in an upper apartment with a woman that he was beginning to fear. The relationship built as Cora listened to Bert's fears and concerns about his then roommate. The girlfriend began to suspect Bert of being unfaithful and began harassing Cora. The easiest solution was for Cora to move to a new location in a small trailer in the northern end of Thames City, Connecticut.

Cora was in this living arrangement for about a year before I began to hear that Bert was spending more and more time with her. In the spring she told me that she and Bert were going to be married in June of that year. The wedding preparations began. They chose to be married in the famous Rose Garden in Thames City. Cora found a white sleeveless dress with a long over-blouse trimmed in heavy lace. Because the precedent had been set that the girls were doing their own weddings, she made all the arrangements for her bride's maids, the reception, and once again, they asked Harvard to do their wedding ceremony. I made her bouquet out of silk flowers since I knew she might want to keep it. I also found time to make the airy crown of little flowers that she wore without a veil.

Cora and Bert Leaving the Rose Garden as Husband and Wife

June 17, 2000, dawned bright with sun in abundance. The rose garden was in bloom and Cora and Bert's wedding was absolutely lovely in that outdoor environment. She had arranged for the reception to be in the Baptist church in Thames City and I don't remember for sure but I think some of the people brought food. My brother-in-law Bud and my sister PollyAnne did much of the organizing in the kitchen since they had run a restaurant at one point when they lived in Vermont. They were now living in the South and had driven up for this wedding.

Felicia made the wedding cake and decorated it for her big sister.

Annie married two years later. There is more than one story as to how she met Steven. The one more familiar to me is that she met him on the internet. She has always been a computer person, so this was not surprising to us. We had met Steven before when Sy would not rescue Annie from losing her apartment. Steven had stepped forward, offering her the chance to come share his apartment in Newburg, Connecticut. I think they had been living together for six months or more when Annie called and invited us to meet them for dinner to get to know Steven.

We went to a Chinese restaurant in Olebrooke and had a chance to actually talk with Steven. His accent was noticeable but Sy and Steven carried much of the conversation. It was a pleasant evening as I remember, except that Annie seemed edgy. It wasn't too much later when we learned why she was showing anxiety. They were going in three days to the Justice of the Peace in Newburg to be married. Then their plans were to honeymoon in Myrtle Beach. The dinner was to gain her father's approval. They were married March 18, 2002, without any attending family, meanwhile, all that wedding fabric sat in my closet! We will always miss not seeing Annie in a bridal dress; however it is not the trappings that make a marriage. It is the loving commitment and genuine concern for one another that makes it a success.

It had to have been about four years into Annie and Steven's marriage when Sy and I received a telephone call very late in the evening from Annie. She sounded strange and frantic. Steven wouldn't listen to her and she was scared. I asked, "Scared about what?"

"I'm scared I'm going to hurt him. I'm angry and I want to hurt him!"

Now she had my attention and I asked, "Do you want Dad and me to come to your house?"

"Yes! And hurry! Maybe Daddy can talk some sense into Steven."

When you get that kind of a call, you drop everything and you go. When we arrived, Annie was in a back room of their apartment and I went in to talk to her. As I walked by Steven he said, "I don't know what's wrong with her."

As Annie talked I began to realize that we were looking at the same Bipolar Disorder that we had seen in Cora. Much of what Annie said to me didn't make a lot of sense... something about her seeing a nurse practitioner who was leaving psychiatric medication on her desk for Annie to pick up when she needed it. She needed it now and Steven didn't understand. As I left Annie and walked back past Steven standing in the doorway he said, "She isn't suicidal, is she?" Steven, by this time, was studying to become a nurse so I was surprised at his question.

"Yes, she is suicidal and in a bad place! Where is the nearest psychiatric hospital?"

"Oh," was his initial response and then he began giving Sy directions.

We drove her to the emergency room and sat for endless hours, Sy concerned and helpless to do anything and I trying to listen to Annie and keep her as calm as possible. At one point she asked me if she should tell the doctors about the voices in her head. I suggested she get to know the doctor a bit before she shared that piece of information.

The outcome of that night was that we got home at four in the morning and Annie was given a bed in the facility. Next morning there were discussions with doctors and she was put into a group therapy situation. The facility decided there was nothing seriously wrong with Annie and sent her back to her home and the psychiatric help she was already getting. I was very upset that she apparently was not being very well supervised with her medications. People with Bipolar disorder should not take their medications in a haphazard manner. I shared my views with Annie when she was well enough to hear me.

It has taken time, but she has finally found a medical group that is working with her in a good and supervised manner. Annie is able to do some volunteer work and comes to take care of me about once a month. –She has a lot of her father's qualities and is a comfort to me with Sy gone.

THE CAPE COTTAGE

Chapter Thirty-Four

Around the time that Elizabeth and Miles were getting married my mother decided that she could no longer manage the family cottage on The Cape and so she had it appraised. When Sy and I heard that she was thinking of selling, we asked if we could buy the cottage. In her wisdom she told us that my brother Copeland should also have a say in this because he had been helping her maintain it these years since my father's death. The outcome was my mother took the appraisal, cut it in half, and then told my younger brother and me that we could buy it, but we would each have to pay one half of the split assessment to whichever older sibling we chose. The result was that we got property and they got money. We signed the papers and were the proud owners of the one physically stable home in my life.

When my mother married she remained close friends with one of her high school girl friends, Marjorie. As things progressed they found that their respective husbands were quite compatible. My mother, Jordan Elizabeth, and my father, Frederick, or Freddie as my mother called him, joined forces with Marjorie and Roger becoming good camping buddies. My first clear memory of this is being in a sixteen-foot army tent packed wall to wall with camping cots and Roger, a principal of schools, dressed in shorts and nothing else, dancing on top of the open cots singing:

> "Sing with me the song of the Jooloos,
> Sing until it shakes your blues loose,
> There's no place from here to Tuloos,
> Like the song of the Zooloo men."

And would you believe--after working on this manuscript for almost a year--I finally remember the last part of the ditty?

When I was seven years old and recovering from Rheumatic Fever, we were camping on sand dunes in Domes, Massachusetts, and the two men had found a piece of land for sale in South Chapel. The owner, Uncle Levi, made a deal with them that he would cut in an L-shaped road if they would clear the land and make it appear ready for lot sales. The price of the land was a steal. Roger, his son Donny, my Dad, and my older brother, Owen, started clearing. By the next year two sixteen-foot army tents went up and we camped on our land with great contentment. About two years later, my younger brother, Coppy, arrived. My mother announced that she was not going to bring a baby to sleep in a crib over a dirt floor. So my older brother and my father set about building a tent floor and the pyramid shaped wooden frame that would hold up the upper part of the tent. They even installed a swinging screen door.

That arrangement lasted a few years and then, one spring, my father ordered lumber. My mother's first awareness that he was about to build her a cottage was when he called her from washing dishes in a basin, and asked where she wanted the front door of her house.

I have dear memories of being up in the early morning on The Cape, eating my breakfast of milk and cereal, rounding up Rory, Marjorie's second daughter who was my age, and we would head for the beach. We spent the morning chasing crabs, inspecting shells, walking the shoreline and making sand castles. Returning to camp for lunch was a must and then in the afternoon it was back to the beach. Or we might spend the early morning walking in the other direction about two miles to get Roger's newspaper and pick up the mail. Today most parents would never dream of letting their children spend a day like this totally unsupervised. Easy breezy summers!

Fast forward to somewhere in the early Nineties: My younger brother Copeland had just married and we had plans to rework the cottage so that it would not be one open room with a kitchen in one corner and a bathroom in the other, but a place suitable for professional renting. We tried negotiating plans for how the building process would progress and soon realized that couples separated by hundreds of miles from each other and several miles from the job site, were going to get slowed down as we tried to communicate back and forth about each move forward in the plans. The solution evolved that each family put money into a pot and Sy and I did the major planning and renovations on the cottage. It morphed into a lovely bungalow which we named the Freddie-Beth Cottage, and several of our children from both families spent their honeymoons there.

By 2004 Sy and I found that the long trip three hours each way every weekend in the summer to prep the cottage for rental was too much. We had tried professional cleaners and they washed the floor by slopping water on it and leaving it to dry. We got to see the effects of the water seeping up the stained woodwork and permanently damaging the trim we had just installed. There were other issues with this arrangement, including a renter that stayed a month. The colossal mess that he left was almost more than two early seniors could manage. With heavy hearts on the part of my siblings and ourselves, the decision was made to put the house up for sale.

It was a great relief to be free of the headaches involved in owning a rental property and you'd think we would have learned, but the smell of water and that soft lulling sound of waves would draw us in again.

NEW LIFE

Chapter Thirty-Five

I've spoken about my passion for flower gardening and I succeeded in making the gardens too large at Lakeview. About a year or so before we moved from Lakeview, Sy and I were out in the yard working on the raised rose beds that I wanted him to build. I needed some of the land rearranged before the beds could go where there was the best sun. As usual I had shown him a rock that needed to be moved and when he got started digging he found there was a larger one underneath. We used to joke that he would ask where I wanted a bush planted, I would show him, and then, once into the job, there would always be a large rock for him to exhume. This particular afternoon he was digging and shoring up, and digging, and suddenly he swung around and sat down. "Are you okay?" I asked. "Yeah, I'm alright. I just need to catch my breath and rest a bit." We didn't think a lot about it when it happened, but about two years later his doctor had tests run and told him that Sy had had a heart attack at some point in the past. I believe that was the day the heart attack occurred. From then on the doctors kept making appointments for stress tests, they added medications, and suggested he have angioplasty done. We no bid most of it except the medications and the stress tests. Sy built my rose boxes and I still have one of the rose bushes from that bed.

Felicia and Chris had found housing in Groton in one of the old apartment complexes. Chris had moved from working at the movie theater to a security job for a large drug company. And it was a good thing because Andrew joined them on March 2, 1996. For me he was love at first sight. Andrew was a bright looking little fellow, dark hair, big blue eyes and eager to move forward with just a bit of timidity. I went to their apartment when Andrew was about three days old to relieve Felicia of her motherly duties long enough so that she could get some sleep. She gives me all her instructions and hands me the baby. Now, she's gone to the bedroom and Andrew and I are face to face. How do I introduce myself to this new wee one? I sit down on their couch and holding him on my knees facing me, without even thinking I say, "Andrew, this is your Grams here." He said nothing back but focused tightly on my face and somehow I knew he knew this was special.

Felicia had a job at a retail store and she was fearful that she would lose it if she didn't get back to the job within six weeks. Andrew was only a month old when we moved from the Lakeview home to the Pine Cone Street cottage. I was able to convince Felicia that if she would bring Andrew to us on Monday and on Friday and then volunteer to work Saturday and Sunday as well, she would have four continuous days at her job with hours that nobody else wanted. Chris could manage the baby on Saturday and Sunday. I still remember the first day when she went back to work. Felicia brought breast milk, toys, pacifier, diapers and changes of clothes. I had purchased an upright soft carrier and took Andrew from her, putting him into the carrier so that his back was against my chest. She gave me instructions quickly, kissed the baby and then was out the door. To this day I can feel his little body stiffen as he watches her run to the car and back it out into the street. I tried to talk to him about what was happening, but I'm sure at some level that memory is still locked within the muscles of his body.

We actually enjoyed our days with Andrew at Pine Cone Street. Soon I was doing the new couple's wash because Felicia could never get to the apartment washer and dryer and still care for the baby and go to work. The Pine Cone Street machines were in the basement and there were a lot of trips up and down those cellar stairs. The high point of the day was when Sy and I would take Andrew in the carriage and walk him up and down the local streets. He liked being outside and would often sleep there when he wouldn't sleep in his car bed.

It was that fall that we moved from Pine Cone Street to Honey Lane in the senior community of Chapwell Hills in Nerme, Connecticut. I have a dear memory of putting Andrew in his door-way jumper and then playing the childhood songs on the cassette player. He would jump and giggle and generally enjoy himself. Quickly he learned to ask for more and then he graduated to my arms and our dancing together in the hall. Looking back, now I realize his soul was programmed for music and you hear it as he is an adult playing his guitar.

Nicole joined us a little more than a year later. Her mother was visiting and feeling very large and ready, but she hadn't received her daughter's name yet. I put my hand on Felicia's tummy and said, "How about Amber?" And I swear Nicole did a summersault as if that was her choice, too. I also said to her, "Now you can't come tomorrow because that is your Grampa and Gramma's wedding anniversary, and if you come tomorrow, I will never ever be able to celebrate my anniversary again. It will be out-done by your birthday parties." Well, guess what the next day was--February 25, 1998! Felicia called me in the morning. "She's on her way and Chris and I are headed to BC&C Hospital. Will you come and get Andrew?"

I think that one of the longest trips in my life was the trip for each grandchild from our house to BC&C Hospital in Thames, Connecticut, where all four of our grandchildren were birthed. The car just could not go fast enough! The upshot on naming was that it was also Ash Wednesday and her father didn't like 'Amber' so he named her 'Ashleigh,' but over time we grew to call her Nicole.

Felicia stayed at home longer this time because, by now, she had been told she had a lot more maternity leave before she had to return to work. Both children joined us on Mondays and on Fridays. Nicole was an easy baby; Andrew would fight his naps in the afternoon especially on Friday. Most Fridays I rocked him and sang hymns to him until he would drift off--or not--as the case might be. One of our favorite hymns was "How Great Thou Art," the hymn his biological grandfather, Harvard, sang to me on one of our first dates.

While I'm talking about grandchildren, Cora and Bert also had two children a few years later. Both of their children were delivered by cesarean section at BC&C Hospital, in Thames City. When it came to the appropriate age for Grampa Sy and I to take the children for visits to our house, as we had with Felicia's children, Cora would not let them come. We put out invitations until I gave up. One day I cornered her and asked why she wouldn't let me take the children and she said, "I don't want you filling their heads with your strange beliefs. I want them to have my beliefs." Over the years she had become more of a born-again Christian. For me it was really the end of the invitations. I regret that Sy did not have as much one-on-one time with his biological grandchildren as he did with Felicia's children.

Cora's daughter was born with a cleft lip and palate. The lip was corrected with surgery soon after Candy was born. She is twelve now and on the verge of having the palate corrected also. She is such a pretty girl with her long, flaming red hair. Her younger brother, Robbie, came several years later and is all boy, blonde, sturdy, strong with a strong will, and a sweet heart like his father.

While Felicia and Cora were busy having children, Elizabeth took a very different path in her marriage. Elizabeth has a strong work ethic and had worked at some form of merchandising ever since she graduated from college. When she and Miles married, I think he believed that she would stop work and start having babies. She wanted to build up some income before that happened for she had taken the money that she forced me to hand over and actually put it to good use. She gave her money to Miles to help the two of them buy a condo. It is understandable that she wanted to work longer to rebuild some of that lost security.

We were living at Pine Cone Street and invited Miles and Elizabeth to come to diner at our summer home to see how well we had arranged everything as we waited for the Honey Lane house to be completed in Chapwell Hills. This was about five years after Elizabeth and Miles had been married. We usually only saw them at holiday time but this evening they accepted our invitation and arrived at the appointed hour. I had planned a simple supper because Pine Cone Street cottage did not have a designated dining room and we would be eating in the kitchen. I can remember sitting at the card table beside Elizabeth and feeling a wall of tension. Sy, being the social entertainer, carried the conversation with Miles but something was very wrong. The whole evening felt surreal. About a week later Elizabeth came to me and told me that she was suing Miles for divorce. He didn't want to wait for children and was off hunting up other outlets for this desire. He had apparently been unfaithful several times before. Whatever, she stated that she wanted out of the marriage and was asking for nothing but her freedom. When the whole process was done, Elizabeth virtually lost everything. I believe, even these many years later, she is still paying old debts.

ONE MORE LION

Chapter Thirty-Six

In and around helping to raise grandchildren Sy and I became increasingly aware that, since we were geographically closest to my mother, we would likely become her caretakers when that time arrived. Before we made the move to Chapwell Hills we looked all around the Massachusetts/Connecticut border to see if there was a community in which we could live happily. From there it would be only a few miles to my mother's home. Nothing felt right.

My siblings had already helped Sy and I move Mother from the house where I first took Sy to visit my mother, to a senior community, Shaker Meadows in Shakerton, Massachusetts that my mother had helped bring into a reality. She was not terribly happy there, but she was safe and did her best to make it home.

In August of 2000 my mother turned ninety years old. Again my siblings, Sy, and I planned a gala event for her, which ended with a birthday party in the Community Hall of Shaker Meadows. Now, reading in her diaries, I can see how touched and delighted she was with the recognition and the party with friends and family. My mother was a brilliant actress and was pretty well able to cover that she was beginning to lose some grasp on reality. By 2002 she was sick with a terrible cold and I spent much time driving the long distance between homes to get her to the doctor, to tests, supply food, do laundry and generally care for her and finally watch her adjust to being on oxygen. Sy was left at home and it soon became clear that a separation was not part of our happy living style. We told my mother in the early spring of 2002 that, since she was beginning to get lost as she drove herself places, she needed to hand over her car keys to Sy and that she would be coming to live with us. The home at Honey Lane was designed in such a way that she could have the master bedroom suite on the first floor and we would flesh out a master bedroom suite for us on the second floor. My mother, Jordan Elizabeth Sanderson, moved in with us on April 28, 2002.

My mother did a noble job of dealing with all of the changes to her life. She had never lived outside of Shakerton, Massachusetts since she was married at eighteen and went to live in the little house that is on the north side of the village cemetery; the cemetery where she and my father are now buried. She wanted to be a part of our family and offered to do chores. It became increasingly obvious that there were only certain chores she could do, mostly because she was having trouble accepting that I had now become the parent and wanted her to do things in certain ways. The laundry became her project and she handled it with grace and style for almost seven years.

Sy did a masterful job of turning the second floor of Honey Lane into a lovely bedroom/office, with a Jack and Jill bathroom, a storage area, a reading nook, and a bedroom space for the grandchildren when they were with us. We had suddenly turned our few years of empty nesting into the sandwich generation. The first few years were comfortable and happy.

My dog had passed away, or, I should say, Cora's dog had passed away. When I found that Cora was keeping a Chihuahua puppy closed in the bathroom in her apartment while she went to work, I suggested that I would be happy to raise Megan, so the young dog came to live with us. Megan passed away at Honey Lane and I missed her terribly. One night I had a dream that Megan was back and running circles around me but she wouldn't let me touch her. I couldn't understand why. Sy listened to my dream and in his way of clear thinking he said, "It sounds like she is telling you that you need another dog." It was truly a magnanimous suggestion on his part because he didn't like messy little creatures running around under foot, although he was always very good to my dogs, if somewhat distant.

I did research on the computer and found a kennel close to where I grew up that had Cavalier King Charles puppies for sale. We made contact and went to see the dogs. From the pictures on the internet, I'd already picked my puppy. When we got there the breeder brought out the dog I wanted and the little puppy began chewing on my sweater button and wouldn't stop. The breeder let several other puppies into the room with us. One quiet little girl started toward me and the breeder said, "You know these dogs are known as 'kissing dogs' but Carol doesn't kiss people." The pup came right to me as I knelt on the floor, stood up on her hind legs, front paws on my chest, and planted a kiss on my cheek. The deal was closed. We had stopped to see the dogs at the start of our vacation and so we put a deposit on the brown and white dog, the one that kissed me, and said we'd be back in two weeks. By the time we got back I had decided that, since my childhood nemesis was named Carol, I'd like a different name and called my new pup, Cara Cozy. She indeed was cozy. Once she became acclimated to her new home, she very quickly decided that my mother needed her extra attention and the two became fast friends.

My mother chose not to become a part of Nerme life—neither senior activities nor the church and I think this made for a very sad end of life. She did read a lot and wrote letters for as long as she could. At first Sy would drive her to the library and patiently wait or help her pick out books to read. Later he asked friends for all their old Reader's Digest books which my mother could still comprehend. He was an extremely attentive son-in-law and she adored him. Over time with the limited mental stimulation, she began to not understand the calendar, time, or the check book. Sy took over the check book duty as well. She trusted me with the decisions for her life and health, but she didn't trust me with her money.

After about two years of having my mother living with us on Honey Lane, it became apparent to us that Felicia and Chris were struggling in their marriage. The apartment complex that they lived in had become a hot bed for drugs and dangerous people. Felicia was left alone in this frightening situation with children while Chris worked nights.

Andrew and Nicole were now in the Grows Town schools. Felicia discovered that Andrew really needed glasses for class work and so they went and had him fitted. He was delighted with his new glasses and wore them most of the time. This particular day he had dropped his books on the concrete steps of the school while he went to play on the playground. He left his glasses with the books. When he returned he found that someone had turned the glasses, lens side down, and scrubbed them across the concrete stairs. They were ruined.

This was the last straw for me. Here we lived in one of the towns in Connecticut with the best schools and these children were being bullied without any intervention by the authorities. I talked with Sy and we decided to invite Chris and Felicia to come to Nerme. We would find a duplex that could house both families. This way Chris and Felicia would be free and safe to work out their marriage either way, and the children would be getting a good education. We made the offer, told them what their rent would be and they were very appreciative.

Within two weeks of making the decision, five duplex houses came up for sale in the school district that we felt was best. We put our lovely senior community house up for sale and settled on a factory-style older home on Hopi Street, one block back from Main Street in the center of Nerme Village. This house would support an addition to make bedrooms for a girl and boy and a proper kitchen and master bedroom for each family.

That was a busy summer. Yard sales, and packing, painting in the scruffy old house and then the moving. The first day I brought my mother to the house, she needed to use the toilet. I directed her to walk across the living room floor that was more like a wash board than a proper floor and she could go into what would be her bathroom. When I collected her at the bathroom door I said, "So how do you like the new house?" She answered, "Well, it will make a roof over our heads." I'm not sure she ever moved very far from that assessment. It took us a year to put on the additions and we lived in the house as it was until the day finally came when we could break through into the new kitchen, master bedroom, bathroom, and laundry area.

I was across the street taking pictures of the changes, when for some reason, I said out loud, "So what's your name?" addressing my question to the house and I heard back so clearly, "Annabelle!" Well, to me she didn't look much like a Southern belle at that point, but I didn't tell her so.

About two weeks later Felicia came to me and said, "Do you think we could put a wrap-around porch on this house?" Then the Annabelle comment made sense!

I said, "I'd love a porch, but why don't you present your idea to Sy. I think he is a little fed up with all my building dreams."

Felicia asked him about the porch, and he thought it was a wonderful idea. The next summer was spent getting a proper porch put on our house and the following year the garage arrived. All this time I was planting gardens and moving gardens as the plans changed. We discovered in a bad rain storm that we had water flowing off the road in front of the house and into our semi dirt basement. I built a retaining wall around the front yard and lifted the earth up about a foot and a half. With plants in that front garden, the water problem went away. As I write I think you can hear how happy I was in that old/new modern Victorian house.

My mother passed away on Easter Sunday morning in 2009 at the age or ninety-eight. I knew that she was close to the end for she had chosen her burial clothes, but she kept fighting the process. We had called in Hospice for the second time and she was put onto morphine to prevent her from suffering as her lungs began to close down. Felicia and I were regular choir members in our local church and I told Felicia that we had to sing on Easter Sunday morning.

"Mom, really!" Felicia said. "There are much better voices than ours in the choir. We don't have to go."

"Yes, we do," I responded. "I don't know why, but I know we have to sing this Easter."

We did go to sing in the services and left Jackie, my mother's caretaker, and a nurse who was to bathe my Mom, while we were in church. At the end of the Easter service we always sang the Hallelujah Chorus from the Messiah. We sang the piece. As we were going down to the coffee hour, since we would also sing for the second service, Sy said, "Give Jackie a call and see how your mother is doing."

I called and got Jackie. "How is she doing?" I asked.

"She's been alright. I'm holding her hand…..You'd better come right now!" And I knew my mother had passed.

My older brother Owen and I had an arrangement that he, as the executor, would take over the care of my mother at the moment she passed. He and his wife had made all the arrangements for the funeral in her home church and my last job was to call the funeral parlor on the far corner of our block and tell them that my mother had passed away. I did so and then turned my attention to the Easter Sunday dinner that we were going to be serving. Everyone was seated at the table when the undertakers arrived. They moved my mother out so quietly that I think Sy and I were the only ones aware that she was being moved as our feast was taking place. Talk about surreal--to watch your mother of sixty some years be carried out to her next journey as you are entertaining her extended family!

Cara Cozy had been very attentive during my mother's last days and now she moped about as she came to terms with the death. We had gotten another puppy for her to have as a companion knowing that this event would be coming. Even Markey Mark, our black and tan Cavalier, had trouble lifting Cara's spirits for some time. To this day Cara will sometimes go into my bedroom and roll on the rug that my mother hand-hooked for Sy and me. She will roll and rub her face on the surface as if trying to pick up the old scent--the end of another lion in my life.

A LIFE CHANGER

Chapter Thirty-Seven

About a year before my mother passed away, Sy was going for his regular stress test and three days later, his annual check-up with his cardiac specialist in Thames City. I didn't think much about it because this format was pretty routine, by now. This time when Sy came home he got busy with some job around the house and it wasn't until coffee time—which we still kept—that he told me Dr. Summers had made an appointment for Sy to have by-pass surgery done by a colleague of his in the Elm City Hospital. We were scheduled to go the following week for a work up with the surgeon and a chance to ask our questions. The week after that appointment he was scheduled for the surgery.

I have always had the belief that once a doctor puts a knife to you, no matter how skilled he/she is, you never come out of it as well put together as you were when God did the job to start. Granted, God sometimes makes mistakes, too, but you are never the same. I didn't say this to Sy because he already knew my beliefs and the doctor told him he would have ten to twenty more good years with this surgery.

We did as we were instructed. We both liked the surgeon who was very personable and an older man with many similar surgeries to his credit. What we didn't know at the time was that Sy would be his last patient before he retired.

The day of the surgery we were both uptight and trying to be brave for the other's benefit. I was able to go with Sy through all the preliminary work up, but there came a moment when they told me to go wait in the waiting room, it would be a long surgery, so find something to read.

I can remember feeling so lost, and alone, and COLD. The waiting room was like ice and I sat and tried to read and shivered for a long time.

At one point a nurse walked by and asked, "Are you cold?"

"I've never been colder in my life!" I told her.

"Just a minute and I will order up nice warm blankets for you." She did order the blankets and that was the high point in my waiting room hours.

We had arrived early in the morning, never a good hour for either one of us, and then he was gone, in surgery much of the morning. By early afternoon they told me he was coming up to the recovery room and that I could join him there in a short time. A nurse finally came and escorted me to where he was in a circular room, sided on three sides with glass, so that Sy could be monitored all the time from the hall and the nurses' station. He looked so sick hooked to all sorts of tubes and plastic bags. His skin was pale, which was startling since he normally had strong color from being outside a lot. They told me to sit with him, talk to him, or read to him, to do whatever I thought would help to keep him connected to me and to encourage him to come out of the anesthesia as soon as possible.

I stood over that bed for about four and a half hours doing Reiki, then resting and back to doing more Reiki. At one point I took a break and one of the nurses came to me and asked if I was doing Reiki on my husband. I told her 'yes I was' and must have looked questioningly at her. "I'm only asking," she said, "because the daughters across the hall wanted to know. Their father has taken a turn for the worse and they wanted to know if you could do Reiki on their father?"

"When I take my next break," I said, "bring one of the daughters over to talk with me. There are some things she needs to know before I can do anything."

The nurse agreed to relay the message. And, indeed, when I took my next break, one of the sisters came out in the hall to talk to me. Now--Reiki will aid the person you are working on to do whatever it is they need to do. I had been listening to the daughters plead with their father to go for more medication, testing and etc., so I already knew he did not want to stay on this planet. I said to the woman standing in front of me, "You do know that Reiki will take the person where ever that person wants to go and it may not be what you want?"

"No! I didn't know that. You mean he could die? Oh. We don't want that!" and she wheeled and walked back to her suffering father.

Sy spent about four days and nights in the hospital and then I was able to bring him home. Now I've told you that my mother adored Sy and so she was as beside herself sitting at home as I felt inside sitting by his hospital bed. We both put on brave faces for our man and he began to get better. His color was coming back and things looked very hopeful. I took him for his post-op check-up a week later and the surgeon told him that he had never seen a scar heal so fast. Sy said smugly, "That's my wife's handiwork. She worked on me most all afternoon while you worked on me most all morning."

"Well," the surgeon said, "it looks like we did a good job and you are going to make a full recovery with no complications." And indeed that seemed to be the case. --Simply a wrinkle in our otherwise fairly happy lives. What they never tell you with surgery like this is that the medications will change and there are more of them, and sometimes, others have to be added to counter reactions from the first. I was not happy about this part of the process, but Sy didn't believe in naturopathic medicine as I did, and I didn't believe in his allopathic medicine. It was one of our few long standing disagreements.

Sy was pretty much up to his old self by fall and back to being an almost full time Grampa to Andrew. Over the years Sy became the father that Andrew needed—the one who listened to the stories, the adventures, and the boy's fascination with guns and history. Sy took him places and taught him things or listened to Andrew share his knowledge. They had a great mutual respect.

I think it was in the spring of 2010 when Sy suggested that one of the limbs on the swamp maple in our back yard really needed to be taken down for it was hanging close to Annabelle, and he could no longer go up the two stories to clear out the gutters. Plus, if we should have a hurricane, we would have damage to the house. I went out one day with my pendulum, which I use with my plants when I want information from them that only they will know, and started asking the old four-trunked tree some questions. It told me that not only did that big limb need to come down, but the whole trunk associated with it needed to come down. I then went to the other trunks in turn and asked for their evaluation. They each said they didn't want to stay if some of them were damaged. They all wanted to go together and for us not to feel sad because they were tired of fighting the wind and the cold. They had been standing together for a long time, as indeed, they had—since 1910 or so.

It was with much sadness that we hired an old friend of Elizabeth's to come in and take down the old tree that really made the beauty in our back yard. Once down, we could see that the old tree was correct. Two of the trunks were rotten and the other two could not have stood the wind by themselves. My sister, PollyAnne, and her husband, Bud, were here from Tennessee when the tree man was grinding up the stump. Bud, Sy, and I went out to find another maple tree to put in as a replacement. I wanted something that would be red in the late fall. We hunted everywhere for what I thought I wanted and we finally found two in Lowe's, of all places. They were on sale as they were the last two maples and we got our new tree for $10.00. Bud helped Sy plant it and stake it and put the first water on. Somehow I knew in my heart that this whole adventure signaled the ending of something, although, at the time, I didn't know what.

ANOTHER ENDING

Chapter Thirty-Eight

Toward the end of my mother's time with us she became less and less hospitable and now, thinking back, I wonder if she was picking up on the growing conflicts of the couple living above our heads. Felicia was either in therapy or looking for a therapist, and she was growing more withdrawn and unhappy. Andrew and Nicole seemed to be always fighting or bickering. Discord radiated from that upper apartment.

One of the last winters on Hopi Street a snow storm was large and by morning the snow was very deep. Sy had had a hernia repaired and he could not go out and shovel the snow. Thank goodness Annabelle had a short drive-way because I was out shoveling our portion of the drive open so we could get the car out for a medical appointment for Sy.

As I'm shoveling, I'm beginning to grumble because no one has come to shovel Chris and Felicia's side and Felicia has to get to work, plus get the children ready and off to school. Finally, Chris comes out, gets a shovel and starts to move the snow. He walks to his car that is not even in the driveway and starts to shovel it out. I'm pretty well finished with my side when he turns and walks towards the house. "Chris," I call. "Felicia needs to get to work before you have to go in to your job."

"Oh, yeah, that's right," he replies. He walks to the passenger side of her van, shovels a narrow pathway, and goes into the house.

"What were you thinking?!" I scream into the cold and silent air. "She drives from the other side!" I walk over to Felicia's car and shovel the rest of it out. That was the way their whole final year seemed to go.

In all fairness, I do have to mention that in the summer Chris would go out and buy fireworks that were relatively safe for children and then, on or around the fourth of July, he would invite the neighborhood children to watch as he and Andrew, with coaching from Chris, set them off in the side yard of the Annabelle house. It was a fun experience for all of the children and something I'm sure they will all remember for many years.

In the spring, Felicia said she had signed up with a marriage mediator to help them make a final decision on staying or leaving the situation. About the third appointment Chris did not show up or provide the information necessary to move forward and Felicia came home saying she was done. It was a long, slow, expensive process for her, but she was free by the following summer. She spent her time with work, her children's needs, and her childhood friend, Jane. She grew thinner and thinner. At one point Sy, Felicia and I were all in the cell phone store in the local shopping mall because she needed help with her cell phone. The young man behind the counter was good looking and unusually helpful, even coming out from behind the counter to show her the answer to her question on her own phone. We watched and later suggested that she take another look at him because he seemed interested.

She spent several months checking him out and making brief connections, but it never went anywhere. Later, Jane and her husband Matt introduced her to a friend of Matt's and that seemed promising for a while, but Felicia saw things she did not like at all and backed away. I think by this time she had become resigned to the fact, that even though she was still young and very pretty, she would be raising her children the rest of the way--alone.

I was extremely surprised the day she came to me and said, "Guess who is on Face Book?"

I responded, "Someone important I would assume from your facial expression, but I couldn't say who that might be."

"Joe is on Face Book!"

"You mean the Joe you were engaged to in high school?" I asked.

"Yes! That Joe!"

Always the mother, I said, "So is he married to someone?"

"I don't know, but every now and then I have looked for him and never found him before," she said.

I was aware that Joe had been pushed to the back of her heart, but never totally 'sent packing.'

A week or so passed and she was ready to talk again. Her friends had challenged her to "friend" him on his Face Book page and she did. According to her, he was in the process of taking down his site when she found him. Talk about the angels at work! You guessed it. Not too far into the summer, Joe was sitting beside Felicia on our couch in our apartment at the Annabelle house. I was so sad to see how much he had been beaten down by the life that had intervened for him. Because I lived with Felicia, I suppose I wasn't as aware of the changes in her emotional appearance. Joe had been a blonde-headed boy with a bit of a swagger and a sparkle in his eye. Now he had a buzz cut and seemed resigned to sadness.

Later in the summer they spent some time with us at our summer cottage on Lake Alex in Dominion, Connecticut, and the sparkle had returned for both of them. I don't think I have ever seen a couple happier with each other with the exception of Sy and me, or a couple that looked so right together.

It was obvious where this relationship was headed and, at one point, Felicia came to me and said, "Mom, I don't think I can do this. He has four children and I have two."

"You're right," I countered. "That makes six kids and Sy and I had five, three of whom were bipolar. I think you can do it." I believe that was the encouragement she wanted to hear and maybe needed the support of her mother's experience. Six teens or almost teenagers are a daunting thought.

We were at the cottage later that summer when Joe finally brought his children to meet us. They all lined up in the kitchen and looked like deer in the headlights, but they seemed clean cut and savvy with a bit of their father's charisma. I think everyone except the children were more at peace after that encounter.

WEAVING THE THREADS

Chapter Thirty-Nine

When Sy and I were trying to find a way to care for my aging mother without removing her from her familiar environment, I told you that we looked for a house to buy somewhere on the Massachusetts/Connecticut state line, but could not find a community that pleased us. One of the days when we were up in the northeast corner of Connecticut, we took a wrong turn and were driving down a tree-lined winding road. As we drove I could see, off to our left, a lake emerging behind the little summer cottages. The further we drove the more lovely the environment became. People in their yards waved to us. I turned to Sy and said, "This is beautiful. I would love to have a little house here! It seems so peaceful." He agreed that the lake was lovely, but we were on the wrong road and needed to turn around and retrace our steps back to a main road.

During that ensuing year my mother made the move to our home on Honey Lane in Nerme, Connecticut. By early August we were both feeling a need to get away, but to what sort of a place? Besides, we didn't have much money at the time. Sy saw an ad in our local newspaper that stated there was a cottage for rent on a lake in Connecticut and he took down the number listed. We conferred and he called the telephone number. The woman who answered told him the price, which was reasonable, and that we could come the next day to view the cottage to see if we wanted to rent it.

We started out and I'm sure were dreaming about the lovely cottage we would find. The lady on the telephone, Noel, had given Sy specific directions and he was following them carefully. I'm musing and he makes a sharp turn that jars me into reality. I look up. "Sy, this is the road we drove down that time when we got lost. And that's the lake out there!"

"Yeah, I think you're right," Sy responded. "Let's see if we can find the lady's rental." We came to a bend in the road and spotted a green and yellow cottage that seemed a bit too close to the road. But that was not the address and so we continued. We found Noel and a lovely lake side cottage set up a bit above the lake. Of course we rented it and had a most relaxing time recharging and getting ourselves ready for a long winter of care-taking. We also got to know Noel a bit and met her husband, Brice.

When the next spring came we called Noel and asked if we could rent her cottage again. Sy reported that there was a long pause on her end of the line. "I can't rent out the cottage you had last year because we bought it and we are moving into it this spring for the season."

Sy responded, "I'm glad for you, but that's not good news for us."

Noel came back with, "I have a proposal. That yellow and green cottage that sits up on the road is our old cottage and we have it up for sale. If you are willing to rent it and step out when there are showings, you can have it for the week."

We didn't really care where we were just as long as we could get to that peaceful water. That particular summer was the summer when Felicia had decided that she was going for a divorce. We invited her, Andrew, and Nicole to join us for a few days. They came and we had great fun splashing in the lake. We found that the yellow cottage and its designated lakeside deck were better for children that could swim because they could jump from the dock that jutted out into the lake. There was one showing while we were there. We vacated and went for dinner. The next day was another showing and again we cleared out. This time when we returned, the prospective buyers had not yet left, so we hung outside in the picnic area to give them space. We greeted them and Sy politely asked if they were interested in buying and they indicated some interest. When they had crossed the street and gotten into their car, I looked at Sy and he looked at me and we said together, "They can't have it because it belongs to us!" The decision was made and we didn't even know we were thinking about it!

Sy said, "We need to call Noel, give her our offer and see if she will hold it without a deposit until I can get to the bank."

I said, "She's a business woman. I'm not sure she will hold still for that even though we know them."

Felicia, sitting in our wide open living room/kitchen, heard our conversation at the kitchen table. She got up and came to us. "I have three thousand dollars with me, which I was going to put down on Monday as a retainer for my divorce. I can lend that to you if it will help."

Up to that point in our lives, we had never made a decision based on something we wanted; we always weighed the pros and cons, coming to a logical conclusion. This time we followed our hearts. We thanked Felicia profusely and I think we both felt that because she was there with the money, this was something we were supposed to do for ourselves.

Sy called Noel and with a bit of dickering on the price, she accepted our offer and we gave her the deposit.

We of course, paid Felicia back when we got home because it was important that she move forward quickly now that she had made her decision. We began dreaming about what changes needed to be made to make the cottage ours. One of the biggest decisions was the fact that this cottage would have to be a regular rental if we were going to make ends meet. I found a website that would help a person advertise their rental property and I wrote the advertisement.

Our ad began: The Happy House is a fully-furnished yellow bungalow located on a small lakeside cul-de-sac. This summer cottage is a little bit of happiness tucked into the northeastern corner of Connecticut. Our cottage retreat affords sleeping for a family of six with a pristine lake, Lake Alex, in full view from the sun room….. We had it rented most every week in the summer for four years.

Unfortunately, as the years wore on, we discovered that we had to be at the cottage every summer Saturday to clean and then to greet the incoming people. Meeting the new or returning renters was a joy. The cottage scrubbing was not! We were able to vacation there in September and in April and May. But even that time was often spent in prepping or bedding the gardens, getting the docks in or out, and sometimes, painting inside the cottage or painting the oversized wooden lakeside deck. The time vacationing there was pure gratitude, but the rest of the time there was a lot of work for an aging couple.

The summer before we had to sell the Happy House, our daughter, May, needed to come home for it had been years since we had seen her. Her father paid for her bus trip and gave her housing. She told us she had only one day to spend with us and we chose to show her the cottage. We also invited Cora and her two children, Candy and Robbie, to come. Over the years and the telephone conversations with May, I had learned that she adored children even though she could not have any of her own. So she and our two grandchildren had a wonderful afternoon out in the lake with May teaching Candy how to skip stones across the water and starting to teach Robbie how to swim. It will remain a dear memory in a relationship that is strong, although sometimes troubled over the years.

MAKING NEW NESTS

Chapter Forty

It was now two years after my mother passed away and Felicia and Joe were beginning their negotiations as to where they might live as a couple and as a family. When Felicia reconnected with Joe, he and his children had just moved into an apartment in Center Town. Joe is involved in emergency responding and the fire department, so he is rooted to his town. The only reason Felicia and her children were in Nerme was for her protection and the good schools for her children. As they weighed and measured the four children with community connections in Center Town with the two children who's social connections were in Nerme, Center Town won the decision.

Seeing this, we began hunting on the computer for homes for them in the Center Town area. It didn't take long for us to recognize that when Felicia and children were gone, we were no longer tied to Nerme or any particular place.

At one point during the time I was taking care of my mother, I became very frustrated and was grousing to Sy and Felicia. In my frustration I said, "And so who is going to be doing this unholy job for me when it is my turn?" Looking ever so serious, Felicia raised her hand and said, "I thought I'd signed up."

With that as a memory we began thinking about following Felicia and Joe to Center Town. Once we took the whole day and drove to Center Town to look at some of the houses I'd found on the internet. Each one had flaws that weren't apparent in the ads and so we began just driving around the town, getting familiar with it and looking for houses that had For Sale signs. Nothing looked promising and we drove down all sorts of small side roads. Toward the late afternoon Sy spotted two stone pillars with the sign Forest North and asked, "Do you want to drive in here?"

"Why not?" I responded. "We've looked everywhere else!" And so we drove in, only to find it was a Senior Community and the Model Houses were close to where we had entered. We looked around for someone to ask and then decided that if the sign said 'Open House' it had to be open. And it was. We walked into this open-concept house where the fireplace was flanked on each side by floor to ceiling windows and sat directly opposite the front door. You could see the columns in the center of the room that marked off the living room from dining room; tucked behind the stairs to the second floor was the kitchen. The large windows around the room brought in the natural light and with pale tinted walls, it had an airy quality almost effervescent. We were infatuated.

By the time we had taken our tour, Melody appeared and was the sales person for the community. She was bubbly and full of information and I felt like I'd known her forever. She showed us the note book of their six major house plans and said that whenever we were ready, email her and she would answer questions or make connections to move forward with our dream house.

It felt similar to the lovely house we had given up in Chapwell Hills, Nerme in order that Christa and her family could be safe as they decided the outcome of the marriage This new community had homes that felt even more spacious, than the one we had left. I was in a dream state on the drive home. I shared what we had found with Felicia and she said 'not to worry'; Joe had a real estate friend who was looking for them and would we come with them when he got a hit. It had to have been about three days later when the call came to meet Felicia and Joe at a certain location in Center Town to view a potential house for them. The house was in a lovely location and not too distant from where we were likely going to build a house. I think Felicia and Joe fell in love with that house. But Joe was wise and went home to "crunch the numbers" to find that they could not pay the taxes on a house in that location. They would have to live farther out from the center of the town.

While this was going on I began working with Andrew and Nicole to begin clearing their rooms in Nerme of things that they didn't need anymore. No point in carrying things to a new house that you never use. That task was no small job because they would get off track so quickly.

Sy and I began looking at Annabelle and seeing where we could start the same process. We did put a deposit on a piece of land at Forest North but could go no farther until Annabelle was sold.

It was in the fall when we got a second call that Joe and his friend had located another property. Would we come to look with them; we did. We didn't know at the time, but Joe had inspected the home sometime previously as a possible place for him to rent with his children. The house was charming and had some of the features of the first with high ceilings and large windows and sliders at the back which looked out onto wooded land they would own. Felicia was tired from a full day of work and this was now evening. I remember her standing in the kitchen, too small for six teens and two adults, and she looked beaten. The house was appropriate and Joe was ready to sign. I felt so sorry for her because I knew it was fear of the future, fatigue, and a marital history of not ever having enough money that was holding her back. At last she said 'yes' and they purchased their home.

Joe and his children moved in December, but when Felicia approached the schools in Center Town, they told her not to bring her children in until the beginning of the second semester which would be at the end of January or beginning of February. That meant that Felicia and her children remained with us into the winter. We were eager to start cleaning, painting and preparing Felicia's rental apartment as part of the sale of Annabelle. As soon as Joe had gotten Felicia and her children moved into Center Town we brought in a real estate agent recommended by Forest North and she laid out a plan of repair and painting. I wasn't happy with some of her suggestions but we mostly followed her advice. It took two months to make all the changes necessary. Then I did the staging. When we finally put the house on the market, it sold in a week. How exciting! But now where were we going to live? We couldn't start building in Forest North until Annabelle was sold and delivered.

The only solution was to move into our summer cottage, The Happy House, while we also prepared that for sale. We had our belongings in long-term storage, short-term storage, the cottage, and a storage unit that we could get to at any time. I don't think I was ever so tired as I grew to be during that period of time. Sy began putting off things that needed to be done and I started nagging. I'm sorry for that because life had seldom been that way for us before.

The upside of all of this tension was that we got to see our new home in Forest North go up. We had chosen a house plan, our lot, and then asked the builder to tweak the plan. We didn't want the conventional white interior trim. We wanted the stained wood that we had had at Lakeview. Five daughters and two grandchildren on a regular basis and I'd washed enough white paint! Knowing that there would be about eighteen people for Thanksgiving and Christmas we wanted an open concept and warm colors. We got all of that with a large eat-at island of granite. This was truly the dream home. The painters that did the painting work have since dubbed the house the Arizona House. We named it the Hart Song since it had a lovely wooded area to the back of the house that attracted deer.

We took possession of the house in mid-September and sold the Happy House a week later. That was a good thing because that was the rest of the payment on our dream home. I believe our guides were very busy through this period because the Happy House had been up for sale at two previous times and this was the only firm offer we received. We took great financial losses on both houses but we were in Center Town and only about ten minutes away from our children and their new family. We began to settle in, unpack boxes, and decorate our nest with the old treasured possessions.

A Bird and the Dragon in Conversation
Jessie and Sy Kessler

MY DRAGON

Chapter Forty-One

Now that we were in our dream home, Hart Song, we talked about how we would interact with the community and I said, "Honey, I'd like to go to the Center Town Federated Church to get a feel for the atmosphere and to connect with some of the people."

Sy, as I've said before, was not one to protest unless it was necessary, responded with, "Okay, let's go take a look at that church."

"I think, since we've chosen to live in Center Town," I said, "we should get involved in the life of the town and not just stay back here in the Senior Community."

Sy didn't answer me and I looked at him quizzically. "I've told you before I really didn't want to move again. But if you want to try that church we'll go."

I think he had forgotten that I already had ties to that church. We went and found the people very welcoming and willing to share information and their time. This particular Sunday the choir sang from the balcony and as I listened, I thought, 'I want to sing with them. I've never heard so many men's voices in a small choir before.' After the service I asked Sy if he would mind if I joined because it would mean he would be sitting alone in the pew without any squirming grandchildren for company. He said it was fine and I went to choir practice the next Thursday night.

We had gotten into the habit of watching television in the evening and that Saturday evening I was watching and he was dosing in his brown chair. The dogs had had their time in the back yard and it was lights out in the main part of the house. Time came to get ready for bed and we always bathed and showered together. I loved my long hot bath and Sy would sit on the brown leather hassock in the bathroom and talk with me until I was done. He'd have a towel ready as I stepped out. Then he would start his shower. He didn't like to get into a cold bed so my job was to crawl in before him and warm his side of the bed until he came to join me. The lights are out and the moon is shining in the double bedroom windows. Sy reaches for my hand and says, "You know, this is the best part of the day!" I nodded in the darkness and squeezed his hand.

Sometime in the night Sy touched me. I'm a light sleeper so I was awake instantly. "What's wrong, Honey?" I asked.

"My heart, it's doing crazy things…I...think it's a bout of arrhythmia but it won't stop."

"What do you want me to do?"

"Call 911, now!"

Sy never spoke to me in that fashion so I was on the phone and dialing. I told the dispatcher that we needed a paramedic and quickly. I told them I thought my husband might be having a heart attack.

When I got back to Sy I said, "Maybe you should take an adult aspirin while we wait. He agreed and I ran to the bathroom medicine cabinet and returned with two aspirin, which he took. The paramedics arrived quickly and asked lots of questions and checked his vital signs. Sy was very coherent which pleased them. Little did they know he was an engineer, trained to be level-headed and alert.

The paramedics decided this warranted an ambulance ride and instructed me to follow. They would take him to the Marvel Emergency Center and then we could decide which hospital while there. When the staff at Marvel talked with us, we both agreed that he should go to the hospital closest to his heart specialist…that was BC&C Hospital in Thames City. So after a long period of tests and history taking, our parade headed to BC&C Hospital. The intake doctors appeared and seemed to repeat a lot of what had been done before. They didn't ask me many questions except to verify that I was the wife. Soon they told me that they were waiting for a hospital bed and I might as well go home because there was nothing more for me to do there. You're loved one is very sick, you don't know what is wrong, and you are summarily dismissed. I, too, am not one usually to protest, so I drove home. Upon getting home it was time to get ready and go sing in my new choir. What else should I do?

In my new church the parking lot is on a slope, so I'd walked up that, then up the flight of stairs to enter the church by the sanctuary. Then I saw the choir was singing again from the loft, so I climbed the ancient, steep, narrow stairs to find the choir's section of the balcony seemed full. The only seat left was on the railing. I am afraid of heights, and by the time I got into my chair, my heart was pounding and my world was spinning out of kilter. I called to the director, "I'm afraid of heights. Can I move off this railing?"

Kimmy responded, "Of course. Sit here by the organ." I didn't feel it was time to tell them about my early morning adventure, but I was churning inside.

Later that afternoon when Sy called me from the hospital, I learned that they had put him on Coumadin to prevent a stroke and they wanted to monitor him through one night at least. He said they had given him medication to try to get the heart beat back in rhythm and when that happened, he could come home. I, of course, went to see him in the hospital and he seemed much better. The panic was gone now that he knew what was going on. Tuesday morning he called to say he could come home, that his heart had stabilized during the night. I was there with the car as soon as they would release him.

At home he showed me the medication they had given him to boost the blood thinner so that he would not throw a clot or have a stroke. He was to inject himself every day in the fleshy part of the torso. Wednesday he was to report to the BC&C Out-Patient clinic to have the Warfarin monitored. I had read the pamphlet that he brought home explaining the procedure and noted that it said to report any unusual bruising. By the time we got to the clinic he had bruises on his torso that were about four inches high and six or better inches across. He had one on each side of his body. The doctor's nurse had us come into her cubical and asked him questions which he answered. I nudged him and said, "Tell her about the bruises."

Sy started to lift his polo shirt saying he had large bruises on his body.

The nurse said, "No! No! I don't need to see those. They will fade in a day or two."

A Bird and the Dragon: Their Love Story

Now this is my Beloved she is talking to and I said, "He has bruises like this on his body!" and held up my hands to show her their size.

She turned to me and snarled, "I already told him they would go away in a few days!"

Wow! What was her problem? But I said no more. She told him that he had to continue the injections until the medicine in his body reached a certain level. He went to the clinic on Thursday without me and again on Friday. When he returned on Friday the medication was at the level that they wanted and we were both relieved. Home free, we could celebrate and I think we ate steak that night. Saturday we went about our daily chores and went to bed early for there was church the next day.

Sy reached for my hand again, and then after a few minutes, released it saying, "Go, do your prayers." I did as he said and fell asleep in short order. After about an hour and a half, I heard that he was getting up, but he didn't turn on any lights so I dropped off again. In about thirty minutes I was disturbed again but assumed it was something he had eaten and dropped off to sleep. The third time it happened, I realized that he was vomiting. I didn't remember him ever vomiting before. I didn't fall asleep this time. When he crawled back into bed I asked, "Are you okay?"

"I'm not sure," he said, and it sounded like 'leave me alone.'

I didn't go back to sleep but listened as he got up about every twenty to thirty minutes to vomit. At three in the morning I turned my clock so I could see it and when he dragged back into bed I said, "Honey, something is very wrong and I'm going to drive you back to the hospital. Get some clothes on."

We drove back to BC&C Hospital in the dark of the night, me driving on a somewhat unfamiliar road and he sitting with a plastic waste basket between his knees. I'm terrified that I'll miss the turn for the hospital and I'm sure at that point he was wishing he could skip this whole part of the story.

We got to the emergency room and I helped him stagger in. There was an attendant there fairly quickly with a wheel chair and we were ushered into the receiving section of the Emergency Room. Soon there were two doctors asking questions of him and apparently looking at old records because they didn't ask me many questions, except to find out how long he had been vomiting.

I now know that as soon as they had him in one of the waiting beds in Emergency, they started the process to reverse the effects of the Coumadin. We waited a really long time alone—he too sick to talk and I frightened out of my mind with what could this be? Finally, orders were given and I was once again dismissed. Hey! It's Sunday morning again. I go back to my choir, all the time thinking, 'If you people only knew what I've just been through.'

Sunday afternoon I drove in to see him and his color was better and he was joking with the attending nurse. They had discovered that they knew someone in common. I asked how he was doing and she said, "He's much better and you don't have to worry. He'll be home soon."

Because I hadn't had much sleep that night, I didn't go back to visit in the evening.

Trying to get work done at home was difficult because my heart was with him, but I tried. I drove back Tuesday afternoon to visit. This time when I walked in, he was flirting with the nurse for that day. She explained that the reason the name on the blackboard was wrong was because she had been teaching an observing student in the morning and had used a fictitious patient name for instruction purposes. Sy was checking to see if he might like the new name better. We joked and again his color seemed good. I didn't take in the fact that he was still in the observation room for that floor. Before I left, I told him I'd come back that evening to watch NCIS on TV with him because it was one of his favorite programs.

I saw a client in my office at home, got my supper, fed the dogs, put the dishes in to soak, and then headed back to the hospital. When I arrived there was no attending nurse around, so I made myself at home and kissed him on the forehead. He squeezed my hand and said he hadn't eaten much because the food was horrid. I laughed and told him that I'd soon have him home for better food. I turned on the television and he drifted off to sleep there in his bed. If I spoke to him he would rouse, but most of the time he slept. By the time I had to head for home, I was annoyed because I'd taken the time to come watch his favorite program and he slept through it. I grumbled to myself most of the way home, but thank goodness, I never said it to him.

Wednesday dawned bright and sunny and I had errands I had to run so I was out and about early. In the afternoon I was scheduled to drive

Andrew to Nerme for his guitar lesson. We did that and I read in the car until he was done and then I drove him to his house at the other end of Center Town. I returned to the Hart Song, grabbed something to eat, fed the dogs, and headed to the hospital, already missing Sy because I hadn't seen him all day.

When I got to his room, Sy wasn't there. I looked around and the desk nurse quickly caught up with me and said, "We tried to reach you by phone during the day but couldn't get an answer. The surgeon wants to talk with you, so please, wait over there in our little waiting room." I waited and waited and churned and waited. Finally he arrived and said, "Mrs. Kessler, thank you for taking the time to talk with me. We tried to reach you during the day. We even tried your grandson's cell phone but he didn't pick up."

I said, "No he wouldn't have picked up because he was sitting on it in a guitar lesson this afternoon."

The surgeon didn't acknowledge my comment, but said, "When we couldn't reach you, we went to Sy for permission to go in and irradiate a cyst on his kidney. He gave permission and when we got in, it became apparent that we had to take the kidney."

"You took a kidney?!"

"Yes, it was necessary. He is down in the recovery room and you can go down and sit with him. I'll have a recovery nurse come and get you."

I waited some more and then this lovely nurse arrived and said that Sy was recovering from surgery and I should come down and help them bring him up to consciousness again.

All of the recovery room nurses were kind and attentive to me and to him. One of them told me to pull a chair right up to his bedside and she started to push a chair in that direction. Another told me that I should hold his hand, talk to him, sing to him, and do anything that would draw him out of the anesthesia.

"Now, don't be upset that he has a breathing tube for its giving him much needed oxygen; but it will prevent him from talking to you when he does become conscious."

There were all sorts of bags of fluid hung at the head of his bed and the lines ran to his arms and back of his hand. I snuggled in as close as I could and began telling him about my day and why I hadn't been there to answer the telephone. That Andrew had had his guitar lesson and was so proud of how much he knew. As the evening progressed, I put a hand on Sy's shoulder and held the corresponding hand. His color was good and he was warm to the touch. Suddenly, I remembered that I knew how to do Reiki and stood up to use that healing technique to sooth and speed his re-entry into our world.

By ten thirty I was beginning to get tired so I sat again and then I noticed that his skin was getting pale. I touched his shoulder and hand. They were cool and clammy. I checked the back of his neck as any mother does. It was cool and clammy also. I motioned to a nurse and she came to me. "Something is very wrong. He's become cool to the touch," I said.

"Yes, you're right. We can't get his pressure back up." I looked about frantically for someone who could help and saw that the nurses were shuffling their papers, consulting with each other, and fixing more bags above his bed. "The hospital doctors are coming to talk to you," the first nurse said to me.

The doctors came and stood at the foot of his bed with their clip boards in hand and murmured things to each other. Finally, a nurse came over to me and said that one of their special doctors was coming to talk and to give me the details. Right at that point he appeared and squatted down beside my chair. "Mrs. Kessler, I think it would be wise for you to call your children in. I don't think we can hold him through the night."

Outwardly I said, "Oh, call the girls?" And inwardly I screamed 'Can't hold him through the night! What do you mean you can't hold him through the night? He's supposed to be coming home in a day or two! Does this mean he is dying? No he can't be dying! We've just started our very own lives together. Oh, God he can't go!'

The doctor broke into my internal anguish and said, "The nurses here will help you with making those calls and if there is anything else we can do for you, just let us know."

'Do for me? Do for me? You've already done the damage! You've killed my dragon!' But again these words were in my head and what came out of my mouth was a thank you for his kind manner.

By now the nurses had me on my feet and were asking where the telephone numbers were for the girls. I showed them my black book and found one number but I couldn't function to find the others. The nurses made the necessary calls. At some point they told me they had summoned the surgeon who had worked on Sy in the afternoon. Next thing I knew, the doctor who had told me about taking the kidney was standing in front of me. He was wringing his hands as if trying to wash off the afternoon's blood and saying, "Ma'am, I don't know what to do! I don't know what to do! I don't know what to do!" He must have seen the consternation on my face at that point because he then pulled himself together and said, "Well, the only thing we can do is to take him back into surgery and see where else he is bleeding."

The girls had not yet arrived, so I said, "Okay. Take him back, but if you can't find it quickly or there are more problems, let him go. It is what he would want."

"I hear you," the surgeon responded. "I understand."

The nurses began to gather and prepare Sy for another trip to the operating room. As they were working, our girls and their spouses arrived with the exception of Elizabeth who works a night job, and May who could not physically get there. The nurses backed away and our children crowded in around him. Felicia and Joe also brought Joe's children, Mark, Paradise, Christine, and Jordan, along with Andrew and Nicole. They each got a chance to say their good byes, and finally, Felicia pushed in to his bed side. Leaning in on the rail, she said, "You know I want you to walk me down the aisle again. But if you can't do that I will understand. You need to do what you need to do. Joe and I will take care of Mom." Later, when talking to me, she said that his eyes were now open and tracking from side to side. She felt he was trying to tell her 'no more surgery.'

We were ushered into the waiting room while Sy was taken in another direction. My almost grown grandson, Andrew, chose to sit next to me and hold my hand. We waited and waited. About thirty minutes later the surgeon walked through the swinging doors at the far side of the waiting room. Andrew leaned into me and whispered, "Gramma, Grampa went in the hall!" The surgeon walked towards me and stood saying, "Mrs. Kessler, I am so sorry. So sorry for your loss! We couldn't even get him up onto the operating table."

I choose to believe my grandson who was infinitely close to his grandfather and knew that out in the hall My Dragon had lifted his soul up out of that maimed and damaged body and started his sacred journey home.

You sit there stunned, broken, in shock, silently listening to the others mourning in their own manner. My life as I have known it for thirty-six years is over. The sun is gone. There is only silence and cold, and tears that won't come.

I'm split; crying inside and thinking the hospital is not going to want to hold onto a dead body. But what do you to do? And then I remembered that my future son-in-law, Joe worked with these kinds of transitions all the time. As I got up to find him, he was walking toward me. "Joe, what do I do next?"

"First, do you need me to drive you home?"

"No." It flashed through my mind that if someone else drove me, my car would then be at the hospital. "I can drive myself," I told him. "I mean--what do I do tomorrow?" Joe handed me a piece of paper and said, "Tomorrow you and Felicia go see Walter, his information is here. He runs one of the funeral homes in Center Town. I know him personally, and he will treat you very well."

Armed with the first step of my next life, I turned to leave. All of the grandchildren had lined up to hug me and say their good byes. Joe's son Mark, a tall burly young man, positioned himself last. When I stepped into his arms he hugged me and whispered, "Remember, I give awfully good hugs." I was so touched by the words of the man not yet my step-grandson nor fully an adult.

On the way home my eyes were mostly dry and I kept chanting, "Life is for the living! Life is for the living! Life is for the living! I only hit the rumble strip twice.

IT IS FINISHED

Chapter Forty-Two

The morning after Sy died I still had to get up from the bed to let my dogs out and feed them. I am lucky in the fact that I don't lose my appetite, even with great loss, so I was going to have to feed myself as well. The day was overcast and cold for it was Thursday, November 21st. I got my coat on and was standing on the back deck while Cara and Markey went down to the ground to take care of business. I'm not crying, just wishing that I could. I look down at the white railing that runs around the deck. This is now the middle of November and there, on the railing between my two hands, is a tiny white baby bird feather. Without thinking, I threw my hands into the air and cried out, "Thank you, Ma! Thank you. You've got him home!" It could only be a sign from his mother, Celia. There were some tears, then.

As Joe had directed us, Felicia and I went to talk to Walter, the undertaker, that day. He led us through all the arrangements and decisions that have to be made after a death. I knew that Sy wanted to be cremated and his ashes thrown off the cliffs back in Nerme. We had come to a final decision about eight months prior to his death. Annabelle, our home on Hopi Street, was up for sale and there were people coming to look at her. We had to vacate, so we went for a walk to our local waterfront park, Captain's Look Out. We climbed up to the bluffs, and walking along, I said to Sy, "It's taken me a long time to get up my courage for I know when you die you want to be thrown off the cliffs into the ocean, but I want to be with you and I'm afraid of the water."

"Oh, that's not a problem," he responded. "See those two trees over there, the ones with the rock between them? I'm close enough to the water so I can still see it and you'll have dry land to rest on." Decision made; I reached up and kissed him. We chatted about other things, sat on a bench and looked out at the water, and then walked home. The next day we were told we had a firm offer on Annabelle.

With Walter's help, it was decided that there would be a memorial service in the Nerme Family Church on December 14, 2013 and then we would wait until spring to have a family picnic and scatter Sy's ashes. A few days after Sy was cremated, Walter called and said he had documents for me to sign and Sy's wedding ring. He would bring them by. I can remember standing by the front door waiting to have one final part of my Beloved back in my hands. Walter came in, documents in one hand and tissue paper in the other. He put the documents on the counter and then held the tissue paper high up in the air. "I suppose you would like this?" he said, and dropped Sy's heavy golden wedding band into my hands. I welled up and Walter put an arm around my shoulders. That following year I wore Sy's ring on a golden chain around my neck signifying the formal year of mourning.

Sy in his infinite wisdom, even in those last hours, knew that the late fall and winter is a favorite time of year for me and that I would be very busy—almost too busy to mourn and so he chose to go home then. Thanksgiving was a week away, and in the tradition of my mother, there would be a family of about eighteen at my table for the feast. I would do the vegetables and Felicia and Joe would do the turkey, bringing it to my home along with the pies that Felicia had been baking all week after work.

About two weeks before Sy died we had written invitations and given them to each couple on our street to come join us in our new home on the first Friday in December for a house warming/dessert hour. Now, with Sy gone, what should I do? He was the entertainer. I knew he would tell me to go ahead with the party and so I called Virginia, the lady that lives diagonally across the intersection from me and who worked with me in the Medfield Pastoral Counseling Center thirty years ago. "Could you help with the party?" I asked.

"Are you able to still go ahead with that?" she responded.

"Sy chose to go at this time because he knew how busy I would be. Yes, he would want me to carry on."

I hadn't even gotten all of my books unpacked and into the bookcases in the living room. Virginia did that, even to arranging them in some order and with some sense of design. She contacted everyone on the street to explain that the party was indeed on and every couple came. Virginia's husband, Arlen, ran the coffee machine which I'd given Sy the Christmas before, but didn't know how to operate. People came with extra desserts, and good cheer, and many, many hugs. Other than my drifting in and out with the intense personal pain, I had a good time that evening. I can't say that I felt Sy there, but I did feel his no nonsense attitude— "get on with it".

The day came for Sy's memorial service and it dawned cold and snowing and miserable. I looked out and realized what he was doing, so I tried to tell him not to sabotage his service because it wasn't really for him, it was for his friends who had not had a chance to say good bye because he crossed over so quickly. It seemed to work for a while. The snow slowed and then turned to a light rain.

Walter had brought me an American flag that the military honor guard would fold during the service and I forgot the flag at home. I told Reverend John about it in time so that he could rescue the situation. I also brought the cookie jar that we had purchased in the Christmas Tree Shop. Not wanting to display the silver urn containing Sy's ashes that is so scary to look at, Annie and I had gone to the Christmas Tree Shop to look for a cookie jar. I guess Grandmothers don't bake big batches of cookies anymore because we only found jars that would hold about two cookies. We settled for a white ceramic bread holder that had a blue ceramic cover. Sy liked blue and he also liked his bread!

The other item that I brought was a bouquet of twelve yellow roses, fully open, to place on the Alter beside the bread jar. Sy and I knew that the yellow rose buds marked the beginning of our journey together and the fully open yellow roses marked the end. Well, the end in physical form.

At the service I sat in the front of the church with Cora, Bert and their children to one side of me and Annie and Steven to the other side. Felicia, Joe and their family were in the pew behind us. As the service was nearing the end there was a stir in the back part of the church where Elizabeth and her father were seated. Harvard is in failing health and so it was a struggle for him to come forward walking on his cane, but he did. We all held our breath as to what he might say. (Remember, he was often the mischief maker.) He climbed up onto the alter, and having the kind of voice that needs no microphone, he said, "I just wanted to take this opportunity to tell you, the congregation, that I was not happy when I found out some other man was going to be raising my beautiful daughters. But over the years I have seen them grow into lovely women under this man's guidance. He was truly a great man and we have all been truly blessed by his life and greatly saddened by his death." There was a hush in the church as we all recognized the resolution and conclusiveness of his statement.

Next came Christmas. Felicia and Joe's children came and decorated my Christmas tree. I had gotten most of the table decorations in place. Boy, was that a hard process because Sy had always been there to agree or suggest a better placement! It did help that it was a house in which we had never done Christmas before. Objects were in new places. I can hardly remember the day itself, except that everyone came, and with an open concept living space, they seemed to all be very much there. I actually have some nice pictures from that day, although someone else had to take them. I couldn't focus that well.

Christmas was followed by Felicia and Joe's wedding. They had announced to us a couple of months prior to Sy's death that they had set a wedding date and it was going to be on December 28, 2013, at the firehouse in Garfield Lake, Connecticut. That was what Felicia was referring to when she said, "I want you to walk me down the aisle again but you have to do what you have to do"--giving Sy permission to pass over.

I had great plans for the decorations--a canopy of streamers over their heads to bring the height of the room down, and of course, Sy was going to be climbing the ladder to string those ribbons. --Joe and I decorated that morning for the wedding! There were also red Poinsettias and the fire house Christmas tree as a back drop for the couple. Felicia stated that she really preferred lavender Poinsettias, but what neither of us knew was that they had been banned two years ago. My florist made up baskets of artificial lavender Poinsettias to place in and among the red.

Felicia, Marion, (Joe's mother) and I went to look for our dresses. Once again Felicia could not find what she wanted but Marion and I found ours quickly. Marion's was a lovely medium blue long dress with a jacket and mine was a deep plumb floor length dress which needed a bit of altering. When Felicia did finally find her dress and had it shipped, she realized that she would be without covering over her top and shoulders for a December wedding. I offered to make her a plumb colored lacey, see-through, shrug-style jacket with long sleeves and ruffles at the cuffs. Marion and Ariel, Joe's mother and sister, took over the refreshments and we had a finger-food feast of goodies.

When Sy died, my older brother Owen was on the telephone the next afternoon asking what they could do. He and Emilie would drive from Indiana for the Memorial Service and I told them not to come. There was no point in coming all that way for a service that would be sad and last for forty minutes. But, please, do come for Felicia and Joe's wedding which would be a time for family fun. They agreed and were there along with my younger brother, Copeland, and his wife Merrily Anne, and our close friends from Nerme, Jack and Katie. And, of course, all of Felicia and Joe's friends and family were there.

The ceremony was a lovely early evening wedding with the couple back-lit by the company Christmas tree. They said their vows to each other, got their rings in place, the minister made her pronouncement, and the couple had that lovely kiss. Then it was on to the food and the dancing. I think most people had a great evening. I know it will be a high point with my siblings because we are growing old enough that family gatherings are few and far between.

In January I was feeling lost, going about my daily chores and silently mourning. The parties were over and I began to dwell on those last hours and minutes before Sy died. I started to wonder if he resented that I had sent him back for a second turn at surgery. He had defeated the attempt but still I could have shut it down myself except that I was in such shock I couldn't think. Finally, a friend said, "I know a medium and she is great. Why don't you make an appointment and go to see her?" 'Maybe a bit of light in my tunnel,' I thought.

I made the appointment and went to see Laura in Nerme. When I walked into her office she greeted me with a hug, then, shook my hand. "Hem…," she said. "You have just handed me a most lovely spirit, your husband." I don't believe I had told her why I wanted to come other than to say that someone close to me had passed over recently and I needed to straighten out some things. Laura went on to describe my husband's personality and things that he would do for me until I was sure he was standing there, at least for her.

She told me that he was grateful to me for making him feel like a man again and that he was concerned that he had messed up our bathroom when he was vomiting blood. (That was the first time that I knew for sure that it was blood. And there had only been a spot or two which I washed off a day or so after he died.)

Laura told me many things about him and things he wanted me to do or be aware of. Toward the end of the session she said, "You need to spread his ashes at the end of April and Sy tells me, to tell you, that he will dance with you on the top of Captain's Look Out."

I said back to Laura, "That's strange because Sy doesn't dance, he doesn't like to dance, and he most certainly can't dance with me now."

She chuckled and responded, "I'm just the messenger."

The end of April was looming. I called my children and said, "I'd like to scatter Sy's ashes next Sunday, late in the afternoon when the park will be beginning to clear in preparation for Monday and the work week. I'll buy Subway sandwiches, Sy's favorite, and I'll bring a cooler of punch. You just bring yourselves and the kids." They agreed.

That afternoon was alternating sunny and cloudy. I hadn't anticipated so many people at the park and we had to wait in the pavilion for some time. We decided to eat our sandwiches first while we waited. Then it started to rain lightly and people began to clear out of the park. There was one couple close to where we wanted to be that didn't move. Joe's daughter, Christine went over in the rain and stood a little too close. They finally got up and left. The rain had now stopped and we decided it was time. Joe moved Sy's ashes from the canister to the bread holder. Each person took a paper cup and we walked leisurely over to the two trees and the rock. Joe opened the bread holder and everyone seemed to hold their breath, not knowing what to do. I stepped forward and took a scoop of the ashes and started to skip around the trees. Just as I did that, the wind picked up and as I dropped ashes, the breeze lifted them up, swirled them in the air and then let them drift gently toward the ground. I suddenly thought that's what Laura meant—Sy is dancing with me on the top of Captain's Look Out. The others followed my lead and soon the ashes were drifting and scattering. As we were leaving the area, the rain began again and I knew by morning he would be well on his way. It would be finished.

It rained hard most of the way home to Center Town. I pulled into the garage and shut the door. As I was moving into the house I heard our girls call, "Mom, come see!" I stepped outside and there at the end of our street was a lovely rainbow arching over where we had just been.

Cora spoke first, "Daddy's saying thank you."

Felicia said, "Sy's glad he's finally free to travel!"

And Annie chimed in, "Isn't that just like Dad to send one last thank you?"

Because Sy elected to have his ashes scatted in a public place he will never have a stone monument, which he wouldn't want anyway. Instead, this book is Sy's monument and his family's love marks the spot where he last touched the earth.

APPENDIX I

Second Chance Souls

This bit of writing is taken from one article that I wrote for "Tidbits from the Couch," my monthly column of the last seventeen years. At that time, my editor felt it was too controversial for a family oriented advertising newspaper and so it has languished in my files, but I feel it is very relevant to the subjects discussed in this memoire.

This month I wish to deal with a subject that sparks controversy. I would like to present ideas that are outside the norm and hopefully it will give a sense of peace to some individuals who are still tormented by their life decisions.

When an old person dies, their soul leaves the body and those people with intuitive sight actually see the vaporous soul float up and out of the body. The rest of us must be content with the unsettling feeling, when at the bed side, that our loved one is suddenly gone. The same event happens when there is an abortion. Often the infant child's soul does not incorporate into the body until just before birth or right after birth. Then, for other souls, they are there from the time of conception. Any of these infant souls that have started to incorporate, will exit when there is a threat. Because the soul is energy, at the moment of the abortion, the only thing that is being destroyed is the body case that houses the soul. So the belief that we are murdering a child is not real. "The child" is not there.

These souls that must exit before birth often follow the individuals or individual that was the parent at the time. It is not unusual for a soul to re-enter the world somewhat later in the parent's life. They may follow the father or the mother's line. It might be a college couple who conceived before they could afford to support the baby, agonized about the decision, but then chose to have an abortion. When the parent the soul is following chooses a second partner, the infant soul joins them because this new coupling still carries some of the issues that the child soul needs to overcome in an effort to evolve into a better human being.

Perhaps the individuals in the original coupling go their separate ways but, later in time, reconnect and bring with them the children from the intervening marriages. One of the children from those intervening marriages is likely the soul child from the original coupling. In this particular scenario, this child will have issues with one or both of the parents. In situations where there is never a parental reconnection, the child will have issues with the parent from the original coupling. Now, faced with the original couple reconnecting, the soul will favor the parent that held out the longest against the abortion.

I am not condoning nor arguing against abortion; I am simply sharing things I have learned from years in the counseling room. As I present this material, I may make it sound as if there is no problem for people involved in an abortion. Most of the women that I've counseled have a deep and profound sense of loss when there is an abortion. From what I have witnessed, no woman goes into this event lightly and for those who try to pretend it is a small happening, they suffer greatly, later. Women are designed to be completely involved in the conception of a child, for witness they lend their body functions to the process of procreation. Like the exiting soul, they also carry scars forward. Even when they conceive these 'Second Chance' souls, there are issues to work through. But I believe it is a blessing to offer these second chance souls a loving environment and respectful life.

I must also note that many men suffer greatly at the time of an abortion. They are not simply lending sperm, they are giving vital energy and energy is not destroyed, it transforms. So they also are soul-connected and emotionally touched by the loss of their potential child.

If you believe you have a 'Second Chance' child, watch for an extraordinary connection to one parent or a strong aversion to one parent. I know from regression work that an aborted child often remembers, at some deep energy level, the events and decisions that blocked their first entry.

APPENDIX II

I believe much of our love story makes it sound as if the blending of the two families into a truly functioning blended family was very easy. It was not. Cora in particular would come up with some reason that she could not attend family functions. She refused to go on family outings and trips to visit relatives. I spent years trying to find out why she didn't wish to come, and begging her to be a part of the family activities. Elizabeth also could be on the fence at times. With Cora I finally said, "You are playing a game called 'please beg me' and I'm not playing it anymore." This letter was the result of that decision and I include it to give the book a little balance.

October 31, 1998

Dear Daughters: Cora, Elizabeth, Felicia, and Annie,

Dad and I sent you an invitation to Thanksgiving about a week ago. Since then I've heard from two of you. (Do you girls realize that you use Felicia as the messenger to bring me news you don't want to tell me yourself, but you want me to know?) I've also had my ear to the ground and I've heard rumblings. They go like this. "Elizabeth is going to bring Tom." "Nobody in the family wants to come to the holidays!" I wonder why Elizabeth is going to bring Tom, when two months ago he was creating hell on earth for her? But I haven't heard yet from Elizabeth, herself. As for not wanting to come to holidays, I understand some of that, but some of it I don't.

Last night I got a call from Cora asking if she could bring Jonah, a handicapped young man that has been to our Thanksgiving celebration before. She heard my hesitation and then I had to tell her that since I'd said you all could bring friends, lovers, or spouses, I needed to live up to that, so I said okay. But I didn't want to. To me, friends are people that make the day so special that you don't want to be without them, and lovers are even more special than that.

That's all background for you from my point of view. Now I have to tell you my interpretation.

For twenty-one years Sy and I have broken our backs to try to bring your two families together, to play somewhat fair with you, to encourage you to talk about your differences, your feelings, and to help you when you were down and needing. We've made mistakes, Lord knows. We do know we 'preach.' But this is the only family we all have access to.

It feels to me as if there is still tremendous rage, anger, unsettledness among you that you don't still have the family of your origin. I believe you older girls are playing social worker by bringing someone you feel needs a family, when in truth, you're using this person to help you avoid relating to the family you belong to. This is twenty-one years later, girls—either spit out what is causing you pain and frustration with your family, or **let it go**! You have been in this family for far longer than you ever were in the previous one!

There is tension in all families at holiday time, because there are so many egos involved, each person wanting to be heard, appreciated and acknowledged as being special. At nearly thirty, or above, it is time you took responsibility for the fact that no one else can give you what you are looking for but you. And if you still need that kind of parental support, you had better get yourself into therapy because no parent can give it to you after you are about three years old.

I attend to Thanksgiving by doing all the physical work along with Sy's help and then I also gather all the undercurrents of competition and put-downs that go on between all of you and I wonder do any of you care about anybody other than yourself? Do any of you wonder what is going on in your sister's lives? Do any of you care that one sister or another may be hurting, or afraid, or feeling very un-good about herself?

You know, I believe in reincarnation, and therefore I believe you are in the family you were meant to be in because these other people can bring you the lessons you need to learn. Blood doesn't really have much to do with who you get for a family. I'm not sure which of you is still blaming Sy and me for destroying your old family, but we were all in on this decision long before we ever got to earth—you included.

I don't think that I'm complaining about the physical work of Thanksgiving, but maybe I am. Some of it I bring on myself with my control needs, and the fact that I'm so easily confused with people underfoot. I'm trying to tell you that I don't want to celebrate any more holidays if they are going to continue to be filled with the self-centered theatrical nonsense that we've had in the past. When we were first coming together we all had to try, but now you are adults, and if you are determined to make holidays an emotional turmoil, let's skip them. You know my dream has been to be the mother at the foot of a table with many happy faces around it like what I perceived my mother had before me. But I don't need it if you girls prefer to go your own ways and make your own holidays.

I'm ready to call off Thanksgiving if this is really what you need. It is a lot of work without rewards the other way. Maybe you need to experience other Thanksgivings, or maybe you need to experience not having a Thanksgiving. But I need to know.

I wanted to call you all together to discuss this as a group, but I knew if I could pick a time when you could all get here you'd only tell me what I wanted to hear and that does not get to what is eating at you. So--I'd like some feed-back on this letter before I go out and buy a monster turkey. I even need to hear if you feel I'm causing the problems. I believe the problems are within each of you, maybe within each of us, but it is time to talk about it, shut up and make a nice day for everyone, or go our separate ways. What's it going to be, girls?

Because if you won't talk straight with me, I'm going to have to take care of myself and vote for peace and calm away from the girls I love. Sometimes I think you would be kinder to pure strangers than you are to each other! Do you ever wonder about that yourselves?

Please let me know what you want. Also, please read the letter a few times so that you fully recognize that it is not all directed just at you personally. It is for all of us to consider.

I love you each very much in your own special ways and I'd like us to have fun together or at least have a pleasant time. Maybe we can't; maybe I have to give up the dream. Please let me know your thoughts and feelings.

Love to each of you,
Mostly Mom,
And Sy

P.S. I forgot the third step in this confrontation—how it makes me feel. I feel very scared because I can lose an awful lot if you all misunderstand this letter and get mad at me. I also feel so sad that I feel sick at the idea of not having any more Thanksgivings, but they aren't celebrations of thanks if no-body wants to be here, and somebody has to open up the subject.

Every one of the girls called and said they were coming. None of them ever mentioned the letter and we had a wonderful Thanksgiving that year and most of the years since. I think they had never done the math to find that they had been step-sisters together longer than they had been in their original families. Sometimes a little well-placed anger goes a long way.

APPENDIX III

A month before I finished writing this story, I was looking up some information in one of Sy's personal file folders. I found this book of poems that he had apparently tucked away to keep quietly for himself all of these years. It was a book of poems that I gave him as a gift on the day, one year later, after he gave me the little yellow rose buds. Before I gave it to him, I made some comments in the margins. Some are too personal to share, but I have included a few here along with the poems, for it illustrates some of the ways we experienced our love.

The book is entitled "Loving Moments: a Treasury of Romantic Writings" and is a Hallmark Edition's Book, Published in 1976.

In the front of the book I wrote:

Sy, October 13, 1978

Many of the things in this book are not in our taste but there are a few that are beautiful--please accept these. I hunted for something that would tell you how much this day meant to me one year ago today. —I truly ended one life and began another—but there was nothing that was exactly right. All I can tell you is that that Thursday afternoon in your arms there was a promise that has grown and grown. It is a moment in our lives I will cherish, not because of the perfection of the encounter, but because of the complete awareness of how deep our desires and commitments were to each other. The encounter has become perfection, the desires fulfilled, and the commitment rooted solidly in everyday reality!! I love you, Sy!

MY QUIET PLACE

The world keeps spinning, spinning,
................the days go rushing by,
....
But, inside me, there's a quiet place,
....
That quiet place is you.

by Francee Davis

This poem is abridged due to copyright rules

And beside that poem I wrote:

> *Sy, this is how I felt when you first turned to me in Group. It has grown even more so as we live together, and if the day must come when I will place you in the arms of God, it will still be so for me.*

COMMUTERS' SPECIAL

All day I function happily enough in second gear,
....
A joke is tucked inside my heart for later sharing,
....

Dusk settles, a half-moon climbs, cars roll in from town,
....
The cat perks up, you come through the door and I am whole.

By Florence B. Jacobs

This poem is abridged due to copyright rules

> *Sy, this is the way my days are spent! It sums it all up.*

THE AUTHOR'S CLOSING REMARKS

First, I would like to thank Sy for being such a fine individual that life with him was simply a pleasure. Thank you for a wonderful time together, my Love.

I would like to thank all those dear friends who listened to parts of this manuscript before it was a book and encouraged me to have it published.

I want to thank the friend who made the initial internet connection to Hay House and Balboa Press for me.

I want to thank the friends at Forest North who have helped with picture placement and formatting efforts and the like. You know who you are.

I want to thank my "first hand holder" for always being there when I was frustrated and for making constructive suggestions throughout this book publishing process.

I would like to thank my children who have heard parts of the story read and never flinched at the exposure, because they wanted the public to know the wonderful man that was their father and step-father.

I want to thank my grandchildren who have listened to me struggle with the discipline of writing and the uncertainties of moving forward to have the book published.

I want to thank my seventeen year old granddaughter, Nicole (Ashleigh Moro) for her delightfully interpretive drawing for the front cover.

I would like to thank John Holland for his Daily Guidance Oracle Deck and Guidebook for I would draw cards from his deck on days when I was discouraged or lacking conviction and I always got the card that I needed.

Lastly, I want to thank all the people at Balboa Press who have guided and helped me through the publication process of this first book.

Printed in the United States
By Bookmasters